GWR THE BADMINTON LINE

A PORTRAIT OF A RAILWAY

GWR THE BADMINTON LINE

A PORTRAIT OF A RAILWAY

KEVIN ROBERTSON & DAVID ABBOTT

SUTTON PUBLISHING

Alan Sutton Publishing Limited
an imprint of Sutton Publishing Limited
Phoenix Mill · Thrupp · Stroud · Gloucestershire

First published 1988

British Library Cataloguing in Publication Data

Robertson, Kevin
  GWR The Badminton Line : portrait of a
  railway.
  1. South-west England. Railway services.
  Great Western Railway, 1900–1910
  I. Title
  385'.065'423

  ISBN 0-86299-459-4

*Front cover: Steam on the Badminton line, No. 5087 'Tintern Abbey' nearing Wootton Bassett
with a Paddington bound express – Colour Rail
'Jack' a Manning Wardle 0-4-OST at work somewhere between Wootton Bassett and Stoke
Gifford – Science Museum/Pearson Collection
An 'up' HST at 125 m.p.h. near the site of the former Hullavington station in 1977 – Author's
Collection*

Endpapers: Both courtesy of G.F. Heiron

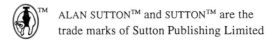 ALAN SUTTON™ and SUTTON™ are the
trade marks of Sutton Publishing Limited

Typesetting and origination by
Alan Sutton Publishing Limited
Printed in Great Britain

CONTENTS

ACKNOWLEDGEMENTS

Working on any historical book has to be a team effort and we would like to record our thanks to the following individuals or organisations without which nothing could have been written.

Eric Best, Sean Bolan, Bristol Museum; from British Rail – John Barrett, Ian Coulson, Gordon King, Lenny Lean, John Manns and Chris Watts; Leslie Bracey, Jack Donovan, Michael Dunn, David Evans, Jack Gardner, Fred Hawkins, Avril Hazell and Jack Slinn of the Historical Model Railway Society; David Hyde, Industrial Railway Society; Mr & Mrs Thomas Jamieson, Alistair Jeffery, Philip Kelley, the staff at the National Railway Museum Library, Messrs Pearsons, David Postle, Alan Price, the Keeper and staff of the Public Record Office, Mrs Saunders, the staff at the Science Museum Library, The Signalling Record Society and in particular Larry Crosier and John Morris, Roger Simmonds, Swindon Library, Jim and Mary Squelch, Steve Tull, Union Publications and Adrian Vaughan. Also the various photographers who have allowed their work to be reproduced and who arc credited in the captions. Last and by no means least, Lyn and Margaret – now they know what we were up to . . . !

The following book and periodicals have also been consulted:

Great Western Magazine; Railway Magazine; Fieldens Magazine; *The Malmesbury Branch* by Sean Fenton, published by Oakwood Press; *Great Western Architecture* by Adrian Vaughan, published by OPC; *The Great Western Railway in the 1930s*, Vol 1 by David Geen *et. al.*, published by Kingfisher; *The Railways of Pembrokeshire* by John Morris.

Not edited by anyone! Could have done with some help.
Spelling at times strange. Punctuation (e.g commas) almost defunct!

The north front of the Palladian mansion of Badminton House, home to the Dukes of Beaufort since the seventeenth century it is without doubt the finest country house in this part of the countryside. The building was altered by William Kent in 1740, who also originally laid out the grounds – the landscaping was later extended by Capability Brown. Apart from its obvious external architectural attractions, the interior houses a fine collection of Italian, Dutch and English paintings together with carvings by Grinling Gibbons. As well as the famous three-day horse trials and hunt to which the house has given its name, a summer drink and of course the famous game of badminton also have their origins here – the latter reputedly devised by the daughters of the 7th Duke sometime between 1840 and 1850. The mansion is set in a magnificent estate which includes a deer park and an approach drive some three miles long.

INTRODUCTION

There can have been few more stirring sights in the 1840s than one of Gooch's engines at speed on Brunel's broad gauge Great Western Railway. It epitomised Victorian endeavour and foresight, marking a pinnacle in engineering achievement. It was a sight which today can only be glimpsed as a fleeting vision so excellently portrayed in Turner's masterly painting *Rain, Steam and Speed*. How sad it is that today the railway gauge in this country is that of just 4ft. 8in., a throwback to the width of the rails on the early horse drawn colliery lines. Interestingly it is also almost exactly the same distance as that between the wheels of a Roman chariot.

However, this account starts with the civil engineering achievements of Brunel, and as it unfolds it will reveal that such was the genius of Brunel that his plans continued on into fruition some 40 years after his death, so providing a memorial to him far greater than that for which he is perhaps more usually renowned.

In recent years there have been innumerable books published on the Great Western Railway and associated subjects, enabling the enthusiast and historian alike to satisfy their needs with books on locomotives, rolling stock, stations, signals, indeed almost all aspects of what was certainly the best loved railway company this country has ever known. In addition there are books, large and small, on the various branch lines and cross-country routes although, there are still numerous gaps which will hopefully be filled by researchers in the future.

Despite such a plethora of books, the subject of the main lines has been almost completely neglected and probably for very good reason. Firstly, the lines concerned tended to be built earlier and so available information is sometimes difficult to obtain. In addition the length of the routes in question and therefore the amount of research required is also a problem. There is also the general lack of early photographic material, although in one particular case this has now been resolved and with, I feel, an almost unique appeal.

Whilst digging through the archives some years ago – and at the time researching a totally unconnected subject – I chanced to find two volumes of sepia prints relating to the construction of the Wootton Bassett to Patchway line (better known as the Badminton route). The result is a unique record of the building of a Great Western line, added to which notes were available in the contractors own hand detailing the stages of work and problems encountered. Add to this some extra research and the result is perhaps the first true history of one of the 'new lines' of the GWR. A fascinating story of men and contemporary technology fighting against all that nature could throw against them.

In the course of the necessary research it has been my privilege to peer into a world almost completely forgotten and certainly one which we will never see again. Here for the first time is the story of the building of the Badminton line, arguably the finest of all the cut-off routes. A railway built without concession to either cost or geographical difficulty – indeed it was almost as if the original Great Western had been improved upon. Eighty years on from the time of its opening much of the original railway is rated at 125 m.p.h., itself a tribute to those engineers of the Edwardian era who were responsible for its original design and construction.

I only hope the reader will find as much enjoyment in the following pages as David and I have had in its compilation.

Kevin Robertson
1988

GWR THE BADMINTON LINE

A PORTRAIT OF A RAILWAY

ONE

RAILWAYS OF THE DISTRICT

Faster than fairies, faster than witches,
Bridges and houses, hedges and ditches;
And charging along like troops in a battle,
All through the meadows the horses and cattle;
All of the sights of the hill and the plain,
Fly as thick as driving rain;
And ever again, in the wink of an eye,
Painted stations whistle by.

Robert Louis Stevenson

The Great Western Railway main line from Paddington to Bristol was completed in stages eastwards from London, with public services on the first section to Maidenhead beginning on 4 June 1838. A little while later came the opening to Twyford and then Reading, Steventon and Uffington, whilst from the opposite end the line had reached Bath from Bristol in late August 1840. Just after this on 17 December 1840 the route was extended west from Uffington through Swindon to Hay Lane, near to the ancient Wiltshire market town of Wootton Bassett. At that time Wootton Bassett was of considerably more importance than Swindon and the railway's arrival was celebrated by an exhibition of old English single-stick play demonstrated by brothers, James and Thomas Edwards. (Neither Swindon nor Didcot boasted stations at this period.)

The 1927 GWR historian MacDermot quotes Hay Lane as being officially referred to as 'Wootton Bassett Road station' although it was in reality only a temporary terminus nearly four miles by road from the town of the same name, '. . . the company are forming it, in regard to sidings, switches and other mechanical arrangements, in the same extensive and substantial manner as is their ordinary practice at permanent terminals'. (Unfortunately no engravings of the period showing 'Hay Lane' with such extensive facilities appear to have survived.)

Until the final section through Chippenham and Box, including the famous Box tunnel, could be completed the GWR directors arranged with the proprietors of the Bristol and Bath coaches to work a connecting service from the Hay Lane terminus to Bath. This conveyed both passengers and parcels whilst a similar arrangement was made for through goods.

The coach service operated for six months, but eventually on 31 May 1841 the

PUBLIC CARRIAGES

WHICH SET OUT FROM THE

WHITE-HART INN,

BATH.

LONDON a four-inside COACH, through Devizes, Newbury, and Reading, every Morning at a quarter past Seven o'clock, (except Sunday), to the Bolt-in-Tun, Fleet-street. Golden Cross, Charing Cross; and calls at Hatchett's New White Horse Cellar.

————— REGULATOR a four-inside COACH, through Devizes, Marlborough, Newbury, and Reading, every Afternoon at half-past Five o'clock, to the Golden Cross, Charing Cross, Bolt-in-Tun, Fleet-street, and Cross Keys, Wood-street, Cheapside.

OXFORD four-inside COACH, through Tetbury, Cirencester, Fairford, Lechlade, and Farringdon, every Morning at Nine o'clock, (except Sunday).

SOUTHAMPTON ROCKET a four-inside COACH, through Warminster, Salisbury, and Romsey, at Eight, (except Sunday).

PORTSMOUTH CELERITY a four-inside COACH, through Warminster, Salisbury, Romsey, Southampton, Fareham and Cosham, every Morning at Nine, (except Sunday,) without changing Coaches.

BRIGHTON a four-inside COACH, in Two days, through Warminster, Salisbury, Romsey, Southampton, Chichester, Arundel, Worthing, and Shoreham, every Morning at Eight o'clock, (except Sunday). Sleeps at Southampton, and arrives early the following afternoon.

*** The above Coaches are in direct communication with the Packets from Southampton to Havre-de-Grace, and Caen, in Normandy.

WEYMOUTH JOHN BULL a four-inside COACH, through Frome, Bruton, Wincanton, Sherborne, and Dorchester, Tuesday, Thursday, and Saturday Mornings, at half-past Eight.

*** The above Coach is in direct communication with the Packets from Weymouth to Jersey & Guernsey.

BIRMINGHAM MERCURY a four-inside COACH, through Rodborough, Gloucester, Tewkesbury, Worcester, and Broomsgrove, every Morning at Eight (except Sunday).

BIRMINGHAM MAIL every evening at half-past four.

LIVERPOOL a four-inside COACH, through Birmingham, every Morning at Eight (except Sunday).

MANCHESTER a four-inside COACH, through Birmingham, every Morning at Eight (except Sunday).

NOTTINGHAM a four-inside COACH, through Birmingham, every Morning at Eight (except Sunday).

GLOUCESTER a four-inside COACH, every Morning at Eight and Ten o'clock, (except Sunday.)

WORCESTER a four-inside COACH every Morning at Eight o'clock, (except Sunday).

SHREWSBURY and **HOLYHEAD** a four-inside COACH, through Gloucester, Cheltenham, Worcester, Kidderminster, Bridgnorth, and Much Wenlock, every Morning at Ten o'clock (except Sunday); sleeps at Cheltenham, and Shrewsbury.—From whence the PRINCE OF WALES, Light Post COACH, leaves every morning at Six, and arrives at the Hibernia Hotel, Holyhead, at 8 the same Evening.

CHELTENHAM a four-inside COACH, through Rodborough, Cain-Cross, and Gloucester, every Morning at Ten o'clock, (except Sunday).

HEREFORD a four-inside COACH, every Morning (except Sunday).

EXETER, (The HERALD,) a four-inside COACH, through Wells, Bridgwater, Taunton, and Collumpton, every Morning (except Sunday) at half-past 7.

PLYMOUTH a four-inside COACH, through Wells, Bridgwater, Taunton, Collumpton, and Exeter, every Morning (except Sunday) at half-past Seven.

POOLE WELLINGTON, a four-inside COACH, every Monday, Wednesday, and Friday Morning at half-past 8, through Frome, Bradley Stourhead, Bourton, Gillingham, Shaftesbury, Blandford, and Wimborne, to the Antelope Inn, Poole, and returns the following Morning.

CLIFTON a four-inside COACH, every Morning at 10 o'clock, (except Sunday).

————— a four-inside COACH, every Afternoon, at 3 and 4 (except Sunday).

BRISTOL Coaches, every Morning at 7, half-past 7, and 8.
Ditto at 10, 11, and 12 (except Sunday.)

Every Afternoon at 1.
Ditto at 2, and 3, (except Sunday, 4) half-past 4.
Ditto 5 and at 6.
Ditto at 7 (except Sunday.)
Ditto every evening at 8.

WESTON-SUPER-MARE, every Morning at half-past 7.

FROME every morning at half-past 8, ditto every evening (except Sunday) at 6 o'clock.

WARMINSTER every Afternoon (except Sunday), at 5 o'clock.

SALISBURY, every Morning (except Sunday) at 8 and 9.

Performed by **M. PICKWICK.**

Passengers and Parcels forwarded, with the greatest dispatch, from this Office, to all parts of the Kingdom

Black Carriages and Horses for Funerals.

M. MEYLER, PRINTER, BATH.

The schedule of Public Carriages from Bath just prior to the coming of the railway, and no doubt similar to those which operated from Hay Lane to Bath a short time later.

through line was ready, and so accompanied by due ceremony the first train ran the complete length between London and Bristol.

Despite the earlier comments as to the permanency of the Hay Lane station a new station 2mls. to the west at Wootton Bassett itself was opened on 30 July 1841, coinciding with the closure of Hay Lane.

Westwards from London to just beyond Wootton Bassett, Brunel had engineered his railway in a truly remarkable fashion with gentle curves and easy gradients, all the more noteworthy when compared with the cruel earthworks of some other railways built during the same period. However, from this point on and for nearly 15mls. westwards through Box the contours of nature dictated a more drastic approach and so

Wootton Bassett station prior to its rebuilding as a consequence of the opening of the South Wales & Bristol Direct Railway – the Badminton line. The view is looking east towards Swindon and whilst the sidings can be seen to be laid to the standard or narrow gauge the main running lines are of mixed gauge. The station buildings are to Brunel's original chalet style and it is likely that the actual architect was one of his pupils. A similar style of architecture is known to have been used at the original Pangbourne and Twyford stations. The brick building nearest the photographer at the end of the down platform is the signalbox and again to an early design, notice too the shunting horse in the yard and the photographer appears to have achieved the attention of the full complement of staff, even down to the dog sat on the down main line! Unfortunately no definate evidence as to the design of the temporary station erected at Hay Lane has been found. Wootton Bassett was the starting place in the career of at least one senior GWR official, Mr W. Packham, who commenced his railway career at the station in 1877 and after a variety of different roles and postings retired in June 1924 from the position of Assistant District Traffic Manager at Exeter.

British Railways

here there are long sections of 1 in 100 gradients, whilst between Bath and Bristol similar natural obstacles were surmounted by a series of reverse curves.

Why then did Brunel engineer his railway along such a tortuous course over the final miles, especially when an easier route was available slightly to the north along the southern fringe of the Cotswold hills? To this question the answer would appear to be that they hoped to tap the lucrative Bath traffic, as well as providing a more suitable starting point for the suggested branch to Bradford-on-Avon which was already being spoken of even at this early stage. In addition a route to the north would have encountered the natural obstacle of the Cotswold hills, which apart from a few minor hamlets boasted little in the way of habitation or industry save for a few small collieries near the appropriately named Coalpit Heath, north-east of Bristol.

Despite all this it must be said that the reasons for the final course of the Great Western Railway through Box must remain open to debate. Was it really necessary to go to the expense of a tunnel almost two miles long when a slight deviation to the north would have been possible? Similarly, is it pure coincidence that the angle of the sun as it rises on 9 April (Brunel's birthday) is exactly right to shine through Box tunnel? Opinion on this must surely depend upon one's allegiance to the designer himself.

However, let us put aside these hypotheses and return to facts, for as is well known right from the start the GWR had the intention and slowly began to achieve the status of the premier railway company in Britain. To facilitate this expansion new lines were constructed, existing companies taken over, running powers exercised and connections made with other concerns, all so as to afford the best possible deal for shareholders and customers alike. In all its business dealings however, the GWR was ruthless in the extreme, its well-loved public image of later years was a product of the public relations department at Paddington, a far cry from the practicalities of earlier years.

Aside from the GWR itself the origins of the later Badminton line can be traced back as far as 1863, for in this year the independent Bristol & South Wales Union Railway opened its 11m. broad gauge route from just east of Temple Meads to the New Passage Pier on the banks of the Severn Estuary. (It was converted to the standard gauge in 1872.) As the company had purchased the ferry service between that point and Portskewett, through communication was now available by rail direct to the ferry pontoons either side of the river, although the journey could still be both hazardous and time consuming depending on the prevailing weather conditions. Interestingly the little company spoke of grandiose plans for either a bridge or tunnel across the river although it should be said it did not possess the necessary parliamentary powers for such a venture. The B & SWUR was operated by the GWR from the outset and was eventually amalgamated within the larger organisation on 1.8.1868.

Neither was this the first idea for a railway crossing under or over the Severn, as three years earlier in 1865, an independent company had suggested a 41m. mixed gauge line of double track from Chepstow to Wootton Bassett which included a 2m. viaduct/bridge over the river. (The route to be taken would have mirrored much of that later covered by the Badminton line.) Much moral support was given to the venture by the GWR itself although its precarious financial state at the time precluded any more positive backing. Unfortunately finance was not forthcoming and five years later the project was abandoned with no work having taken place.

But the GWR were not prepared to allow the ideal of improved communications between Bristol and South Wales to lapse and so in 1872, having recovered from their earlier financial embarrassment, the crossing of the River Severn was again raised at board level. According to MacDermot the moving spirit was none other than Sir Daniel Gooch himself, but the proposal this time was for a tunnel rather than a bridge. Leading the campaign was Charles Richardson who had been the resident GWR engineer during the construction of the B & SWUR.

It should be mentioned at this stage that the need for a Severn crossing was based upon a requirement for improved communications with the rapidly expanding coal mining industry within the South Wales area. The area's pits had recorded a rise in output of between ½ million to 2 million tons per annum from about 1865 onwards, so that by the mid-1880s annual output from the coalfields was put at no less than 20.2 million tons per annum. The South Wales area is also recorded as having produced the largest growth rate anywhere in the country as regards both workforce and industrial output during the period in question. Much of this coal was for export, although large quantities were also destined for the London market as well as the South Coast ports. Therefore improved transport which avoided the long haul via Gloucester was thus seen as an important consideration.

The GWR funded Severn tunnel was finally completed and opened for traffic in 1886. It was a colossal engineering feat in itself and its completion was due in no small part to the backing of Gooch. It may be said that its construction and continued existence remains as a memorial to Gooch himself, even if it is a less obvious one when compared with the works of his contemporary, Brunel. It was also really the first in the redevelopment programme of new lines that would carry the company through to the end of its independent life.

The Severn tunnel railway connected into the former B & SWUR at Pilning, although at the time the tunnel was opened the former 'Union line was for part of its course still single track. Doubling was finally completed in 1887 and included the famous section between Patchway and Pilning where the up and down lines traversed different levels. This was necessary so as to provide a slightly easier 1 in 100 gradient compared with the original 1 in 68 alignment. Coinciding with the opening of the Severn tunnel the line from Pilning to New Passage together with the ferry service was abandoned, although part of the old railway was resurrected in 1900 in the new Pilning–Avonmouth line.

With the opening of the Severn tunnel the GWR now had a relatively direct route from South Wales to London so avoiding the 'Great Way Round' from Newport via Gloucester. The former B & SWUR joined the original main line just west of Temple Meads at Bristol by means of a triangular junction, which also allowed trains to reach the West Country without reversal.

Coal traffic for London and the south still faced the disadvantages of the various curves and gradients from Bristol through Bath to Wootton Bassett. But for the time being it was still an improvement even if history would record it to be a short-lived one.

Elsewhere on the system the GWR were slowly ridding themselves of the legacy of Brunel's broad gauge. Magnificent though the broad gauge undoubtably was, its *tedly* downfall was due to purely economic reasons – the potential today for a broad gauge high speed passenger service can only be imagined. Accordingly the Severn tunnel had from the outset been designed as a standard gauge project, with the broad gauge being banished from South Wales as early as 1872, twenty years before its final demise on the main line to the West Country via Bristol.

With reference to the railways of South Wales it must be said that here the GWR certainly did not enjoy a general monopoly of traffic as it did in so many other places. Instead there were a number of small companies whose main trade was the transport of coal from the collieries down the valleys to the docks, which besides competing with each other crossed and re-crossed the GWR. From the amount of trade carried most were highly profitable; the Barry Railway was even reputed to have so much money to spare that it contemplated changing all of its rail chairs from cast iron to brass and a number of these were allegedly provided. It was these small but powerful South Wales railway companies that would play such an important part in the development of the Badminton line project later on.

Apart from its railway commitments, the GWR was very keen to develop its dealings in both shipping and dock operation. The former had commenced back in 1872 when the City of Bristol had looked to the GWR to develop the port of Avonmouth. But the railway had other ideas, preferring Fishguard, almost the furthest point west on mainland Wales which it considered as being more suitable. There were several reasons for this, one being that here the GWR would be unlikely to have any competition from another concern, unlike Plymouth for example where the L & SWR already had a hold. More important however was a saving in nautical miles for the liner traffic, 135mls. compared with Liverpool and 200mls. compared with Southampton – the latter equal to almost one day extra at sea.

But in speaking of Fishguard in this way we have jumped ahead some years as the little town did not receive its first railway until 1899 and even then by an independent company. There was also a political undercurrent within the railway organisation which had it that the rival London and North Western might attempt to secure access to the port and so armed with this information the GWR lost no time in seeking to buy out the independent North Pembrokeshire & Fishguard Railway which it did even before the final section from Letterston to Fishguard was opened to traffic.

No time was wasted either in developing the area with a magnificent new harbour and rail facilities, again superb engineering achievements in themselves. A new rail line to the port was also built from Clarbeston Road whilst the Irish ferry service was switched from Neyland. The railway publicists seized upon the venture decribing Fishguard as '. . . The Gateway to Europe . . .', although it does not take an extensive geographical knowledge to realise that such a claim was somewhat excessive. But Fishguard did have something to offer, for by disembarking from a transatlantic liner at the port the travelling time to London could be reduced to five hours, it was

Part of the vast new facilites provided by the GWR at Fishguard with the intention of capturing both passenger and freight traffic from the Atlantic liners as well as the ferry services to Southern Ireland. From the latter large quantities of cattle were received, hence the number of 'Mex' vans in the sidings. The main running lines are on the right, the roof of the passenger station is just discernable in the background.

British Railways

also seen as a direct rival to the LNWR's packet traffic to Ireland emanating from Holyhead.

To the GWR the culmination of this dream must surely have come in 1909 when Cunard's *Mauretania*, then the largest liner afloat, began to make regular calls on her North Atlantic schedule. Brunel's dream of the Great Western Railway linking London with New York had drawn another step closer.

Unfortunately such success was short-lived, as with the outbreak of the First World War such traffic was abruptly curtailed never to return. Instead Fishguard would continue in its single role as the GWR's sole shipping route to Ireland, a sad reminder of what might have been possible. Once again though we have jumped in time, although this is perhaps preferable to jumping geographically around the railway system. A mention of a direct line to Fishguard has already been made, whilst elsewhere the question of an easier route to the area was under active consideration.

In particular the section through Bath and Bristol came under scrutiny, and it was not long before the idea of a direct new route from the Severn Tunnel was suggested. The ideal starting point was Wootton Bassett and a new railway linking the two named locations would serve the following needs:

A shorter line to South Wales with easier gradients for coal traffic;
A faster line to Bristol by avoiding Bath;
Easier access to Fishguard for the liner traffic;
Reduced congestion west of Wootton Bassett.

The first point was of particular relevance as within South Wales the powerful little independent lines were already making threatening noises over the roundabout route for coal traffic via Bath. So much so that in the early 1890s the Barry company was openly speaking of building an independent line all the way to London, 163mls. long, complete with its own rival Severn Tunnel. The cost of this route was put as in excess of £5 million. Although, publically at least, the GWR appeared to take little notice of such threats, they did let it be known that a more direct approach was receiving serious consideration.

Behind the scenes however it was a different story, for Paddington had wasted little time in undertaking a full survey of a proposed route which would run almost due west from Wootton Bassett, through the southernmost fringe of the Cotswold ridge to a junction near Patchway. The estimated cost was put at £1,116,348. 9s. 6d.[1] It was noted that a number of properties would require demolishing in the vicinity of Old Sodbury to make room for the railway:

In Church Lane, 2 cottages at present occupied by 8 persons.
In Main Road Sodbury Village, 8 cottages at present occupied by
    32 persons.
In Doddington or Chapel Lane, 10 cottages at present occupied by
    29 persons.

Altogether this can well be considered to be a small disruption considering the length of the line and only goes to show the rural nature of the route chosen.

By the end of 1895 a decision had been made and board approval was given for the new route as surveyed. It was to be the longest and most lavish of all the cut-offs the GWR had constructed, and while today one may doubt the wisdom of building such a

1.   As was the general practice in civil engineering terms a 10% contingency was later added to cover unforeseen costs and thus helps to explain the jump of £1.3 million mentioned later. The figures are taken from one of the few surviving authentic GWR documents on the finances for the period. PRO Ref; RAIL 1066/769.

route, especially in view of the short life of Fishguard as a world port, it must be remembered that in the 1890s all this was in the future. It was a future which looked nothing but rosy, as indicated by the General Manager of the GWR, J.L. Wilkinson when he was initially questioned on the subject of London suburban traffic by G.A. Sekon, the first editor of the *Railway Magazine*; with the following result:

> Sekon – 'You have other possibilities of expansion of traffic within the range of practical politics I presume Mr Wilkinson?'
>
> Wilkinson – 'Certainly, for instance, sooner or later – and perhaps sooner than many expect – Milford will become the port for dealing with an extensive overseas traffic, which when the time comes the Great Western Railway will be glad to accommodate. When the time comes, it is possible that the Paddington–Milford boat specials may be the "crack" trains of the world.'

This, however, was merely the projected public image, as unbeknown to the readers of the *Railway Magazine* behind the scenes plans for the rival line were almost ready to be laid before Parliament. This was for a 'London & South Wales Railway', promoted by the Barry Company and so providing a line from Cardiff direct to a link with the Metropolitan and Midland Companies at Hendon in north London. The new route was also very close to the projected GWR-backed line as it would have passed through the town of Malmesbury only some 3mls. north of what was later Little Somerford station.

The Bill for the GWR new line was laid before Parliament on 9 November 1895 and attracted a number of objectors. Amongst these were Sarah Brown and the Rev. Richard Brown of The Rectory, Old Sodbury whose complaint concerned the loss of property – history unfortunately fails to record if this was their own habitat or perhaps some of the cottages referred to above. Then there was Robert Tanner of Kingsmead Mill, Little Somerford who was concerned that the proposed new railway embankment would seriously affect the water supply to his mill. There were also objections from a number of local landowners as well from the County Councils of Gloucestershire and Wiltshire although again the grounds for these complaints are not recorded.

Just three weeks later on 30 November 1895 the Barry Railway's bill was also submitted to Parliament and of course was in direct opposition to the GWR scheme. Fortunately common sense prevailed and after some behind the scenes negotiations, the London & South Wales proposal was withdrawn, leaving the way clear for the Great Western. As to whether the Barry company's proposal was merely a political gesture to force the hand of the GWR is unclear and the whole question of a rival line must forever remain conjecture.

The GWR Act specified that the course was to be almost exactly that originally intended, with most of the route through virgin territory as far as existing lines were concerned. Indeed over the complete distance of more than 30mls. there were only two lines to be crossed, the first, the somewhat insignificant GWR branch line from Dauntsey to its terminus at Malmesbury, and the second a line of far more importance, the Midland Railway main line from Gloucester to Bristol. The Act also

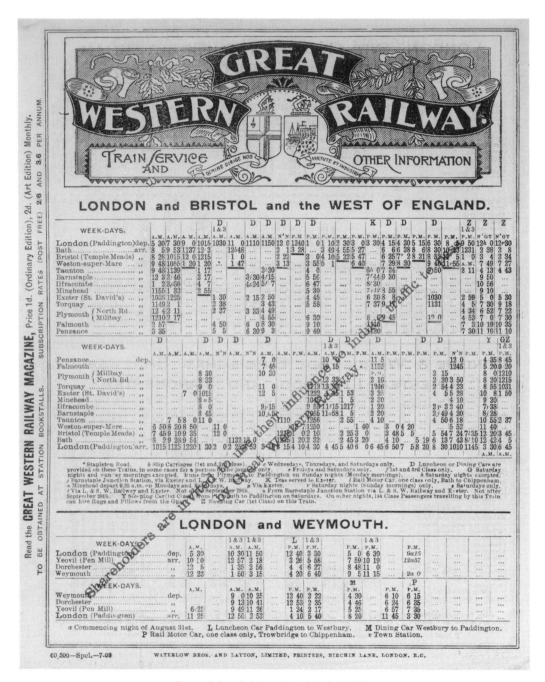

Copy of shareholders timetable, July 1908.

included a number of connecting lines from the new route to the MR and these are discussed in detail later in the text.

Surprisingly there is little mention of any objections from the MR themselves, although it is fairly certain that there would have been some. Instead a number of separate agreements were reached between the two companies for connecting lines and spurs where the MR would pass under the new route at Westerleigh. (These are referred to in detail in the section on the appropriate route.)

As a result of the difficulties with the industrialists in South Wales, the GWR (South Wales & Bristol Direct Railway) Act was authorised on 7 August 1896. A separate agreement of 23 July 1896 with the Midland Railway related to the withdrawal from the Bill of a 'Railway No. 2' in the proposal, substituting instead connecting loops at Westerleigh, Berkeley and Standish Junction together with the requisite running powers. The changes agreed with the Midland Railway, and put into effect only a matter of two weeks before the Bill received the Royal Assent meant that in the schedule of the new Act the connecting lines to the Midland had been hastily rearranged. (A number of the relevant clauses from the Act are reproduced on p. 14.)

What the legal niceties do not convey is the sheer magnitude of the new line, described by a contemporary writer in the *Railway Magazine* as '. . . one of the greatest undertakings of the GWR not excepting the abolition of the broad gauge . . .', and involving 5,000,000cu.yds of excavation as well as 88 bridges, 2 tunnels and 4 viaducts. Indeed everything for the new line was on a grand scale and truely followed in the Brunel tradition. No curves of less than 1m. radius and no gradient steeper than 1 in 300. In this way the new route followed in almost exactly the same manner as the main line from London; indeed, to the west it avoided the steep gradients and sharp curves of Box and Bath but at the cost of considerable earthworks on crossing the lower reaches of the Cotswolds.

The Act also provided other useful information as to the negotiations and concessions that took place with the various landowners away from the public gaze. One example was that of Sir Algernon William Neeld, Baronet, who insisted that the new line be carried across his land at Alderton in a tunnel instead of the cutting as originally intended. Five years[2] were allowed for completion of the work but the powers for compulsory purchase expired after three years.

---

2. Section 17 of the GWR (South Wales and Bristol Direct Railway) Act of 1896 provides as follows:

> If the company fail within the period limited by this Act to complete the railways the Company shall be liable to a penalty of fifty pounds a day for every day after the expiration of the period so limited until the railways are completed and opened for the public conveyance of passengers or until the sum received in respect of such penalty shall amount to five per centum on the estimated cost of the uncompleted railway or railways; The said penalty may be applied for by any landowner or other claiming to be compensated or interested . . .

As the line was not finally opened to passengers until 1.7.1903 it may be assumed that a penalty on 695 days was accrued which would have amounted to £34,750. Not surprisingly official records make no mention of any such penalty being paid!

The cost of the new route was now estimated at [to be] in excess of £1.3 million, a considerable figure at that time. The Act allowed the GWR to raise only slightly less than half of this, a mere £600,000 in new capital. It is interesting to note that the difference between the capital authorised to be raised and the final estimate was funded direct [directly] from the GWR reserve account, despite coming at a time when the company had numerous other large projects under way. Whether this had been the original intention or was forced upon the company by Parliament is unclear. Of the total cost of the new project, land purchases alone were estimated to account for some £200,000, itself a revealing assessment of the value of a narrow strip of land through the southern fringe of the Cotswolds even in the last century. The conclusion drawn from this must be that an element in this figure must be taken to be 'compensation' rather than a straight reimbursement, as based on the length of the railway the average cost of land works out at in excess of £6779 per linear mile.

The funding is in itself a particularly noteworthy feature, for within recent years a considerable amount of investment had already been made in the abolitition of the broad gauge, and in addition plans were afoot for additional new cut-off lines and works elsewhere on the system. These included the Stert & Westbury line authorised in 1894, and within the next few years work would commence on the final link in the new fast route to Devon and Cornwall via Westbury as well as the direct line to Birmingham through High Wycombe. They were all developments designed to revive the company ready to meet the challenge the new century presented as well as to remove its image as the 'Great Way Round'. This new work was only possible due to a rapid rise in receipts from 1884 onwards which were equal to an increase of 37% from 1882 to 1894, with a further 23% increase from 1894 to 1900. It is small wonder that such traffic, new lines, locomotives and rolling stock provided the Edwardian era with the fitting title 'The Golden Age of Railway Travel'.

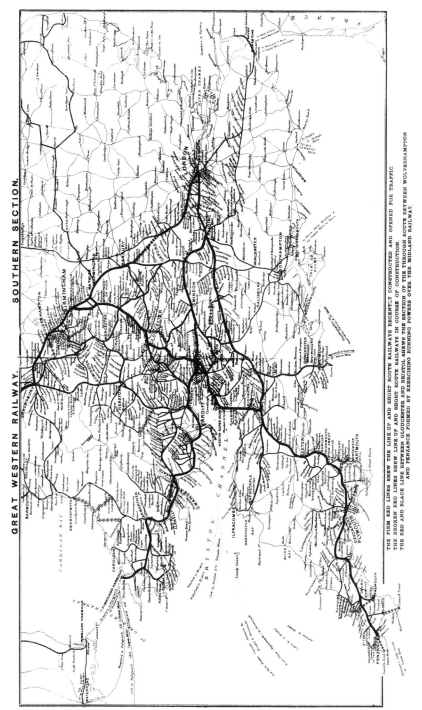

A GWR map as issued to shareholders in 1908. The original is printed in black with the new lines and cut-offs picked out in red. From the routes shown it is easy to identify the importance of the new Badminton line in relation to the direct route from Paddington to Fishguard. The timetable was sent out with the half-yearly dividend warrants and included the following addition in red across the front cover; 'Shareholders are invited to use their influence to induce traffic to pass by Great Western Railway.' Perhaps surprisingly there is no direct reference to the new line within the timetable itself.

SECTIONS OF THE ACT OF 1896

1.   A Railway (No. 1) 21 miles 4 furlongs and 3.50 chains in length commencing in the parish of Wootton Bassett by a junction with the Main Line of Railway of the Company and terminating in the parish of Old Sodbury near the Bell Inn Old Sodbury.

2.   A Railway (in the deposited Plans Section and Books of Reference referred to as Railway No. 3) 8 miles 4 furlongs and 5.85 chains in length commencing in the parish of Old Sodbury by a junction with Railway No. 1 at its termination and terminating in the parish of Stoke Gifford by a junction with the Bristol and South Wales Union Railway of the Company.

3.   A Railway (in the deposited Plans Sections and Books of Reference referred to as Railway No. 4) 7 furlongs and 9.50 chains in length commencing in the parish of Stoke Gifford by a junction with Railway No. 3 and terminating in the parish of Filton by a junction with the said Bristol and South Wales Union Railway.

4.   A Railway to be called the Midland Junction Railway No. 1a, 1 mile 3 furlongs and 6.50 chains in length commencing in the Parish of Wapley and Codrington in the County of Gloucester by a junction with Railway No. 3 by this Act authorised and terminating in the Parish of Westerleigh by a junction with the Bristol and Gloucester Railway of the Midland Company.

5.   A Railway to be called the Midland Junction Railway No. 2a, 6 furlongs and 2.20 chains in length commencing by a junction with the Midland Junction Railway No. 1a by this Act authorised and terminating by a junction with the said Bristol and Gloucester Railway.

6.   A Railway to be called the Midland Junction Railway No. 3a, 3 furlongs and 8.60 chains in length commencing by a junction with the Midland Junction Railway No. 1a by this Act authorised and terminating by a junction with Railway No. 3 by this Act authorised.

7.   A Railway to be called the Berkeley Road Junction Railway, 1 mile 2 furlongs and 6.40 chains in length commencing by a junction with the said Bristol and Gloucester Railway and terminating by a junction with the Berkeley New Docks Branch of the Company and the Midland Railway.

8.   A Railway to be called the Stonehouse Junction Railway 5 furlongs and 5.75 chains in length commencing by a junction with the said Bristol and Gloucester Railway and terminating by a junction with the Railway of the Company.

Excavation of the new line using a Ruston & Procter 'steam navvy'. Seventeen machines of similar type were in use on the new line.

Railway Magazine

a temporary connection at Wootton Bassett and an overland road was also extended as far as 1m, 10ch. which was used for supplies. There is also a reference to plant and supplies being brought from Somerford, '. . . as may be found most advantageous'. A connection off the Malmesbury branch from Dauntsey was also provided, this is believed to have been used for the first time in mid-October 1897. For the contractors, Mr Ernest Pearson and Mr G. Hay were in charge of the works, assisted by Messrs Colson, Gripper, Hyne and Manton.

On No. 1 section the first work to be started was the fencing of the route. This was begun on 20 December 1897 and proceeded at the rate of approximately a mile per week. For this first section two steam navvies from the previous contract at Maesteg on the Port Talbot Railway were brought in for use on the numerous heavy earthworks involved. It was also estimated that five standard gauge steam engines together with 120 wagons would be required along with one 3ft. gauge engine with 50 wagons. The contractors engines ran on rail of a nominal 56lb./yd. linear weight which was laid on wooden sleepers, this applied to both the standard and 3ft. gauge lines. Finally a portable steam crane was brought in from Cardiff along with a number of hand derricks.

The use of the narrow gauge stock was confined to cuttings Nos. 5 and 7 (just west of Brinkworth). No. 7 was started first and was due for completion around August 1898, after which work would start on cutting No. 5. Why the narrow gauge equipment was used is unclear, although it may have been difficulties with the ground or simply a shortage of standard gauge equipment.

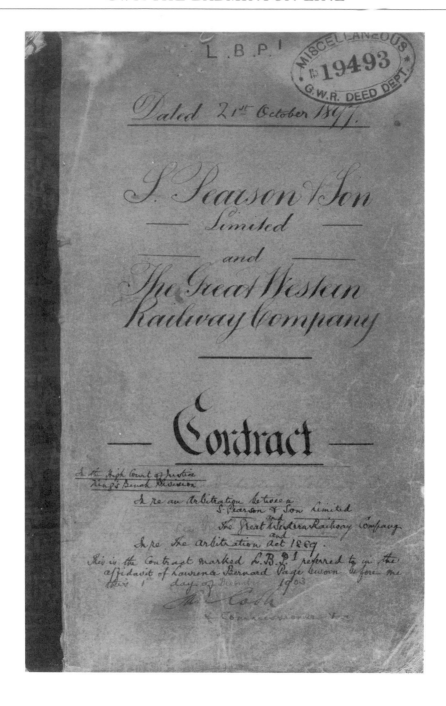

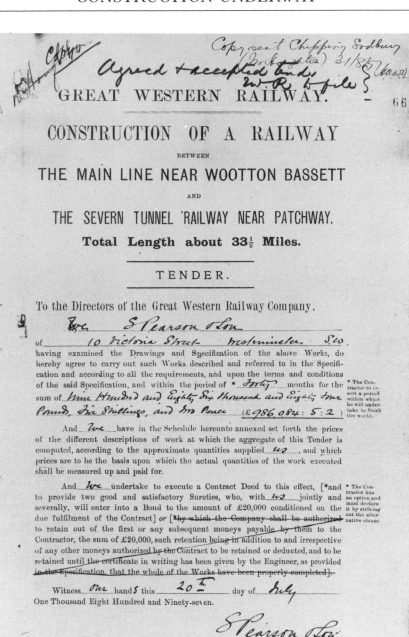

Courtesy of B.R. Archives.

A short 176yd. tunnel had originally been proposed on the first section but this was substituted with an open cutting with slopes at 1 in 5. The major engineering feat was an embankment extending almost 5mls. from beyond Brinkworth and for which 1 million cu.yds. of spoil were required.

It was clear from the start that Pearson's operated to a strict timetable for the works. The following references to cuttings Nos. 1 and 3 are indicative of this criteria:

Cutting 1. (West end) to be started as soon as fencing has been fixed with barrows and hand carts running the material into Bank 2. This bank must be completed by the time Steam Navvy has finished at east end of cutting 1 and the whole of cutting 2, viz in 10 weeks from January 10th . . .

Cutting 2. Start at each end with barrows and hand carts as soon as the fencing has been erected giving the east the preference so as to assist in filling bank 2 as soon as possible.

Cutting 3. Start No. 2 Steam Navvy at East end 2m. 20ch. March 1st. and work into Bank 3. A minimum quantity of 10,000 (cu.yds) per month must be done and if not completed work must be suspended as soon as Winter sets in say October 31st 1898 but an effort must be made either by working 1 time or night work during favourable months to complete this cutting by the time named. Slopes must be trimmed as close up to the face as possible both in this and all other cutting on the section so as to minimise the risk of slips.

Cutting 4. To be worked in two lifts. The No. 1 navvy to be sent from cutting 1 (west end) after completing that cutting up to tunnel end. This should be started on or before July 1st. but not later in top lift of cutting working Bank 4 as long as weather permits say, until Oct. 31st. 1898 when work will be discontinued until Spring in the following year. The whole cutting to be finished before Autumn 1899. Nos. 1 & 2 navvies being employed from Spring 1899 until completion of this cutting in Autumn the same year.

Further reports continue and then there is an interesting reference under Cutting 7:

West end to be worked by narrow gauge plant and tipped into bank 8. The loco *Brancker* to be employed after it has finished on No. 2 section which is expected to be not later than April 1898.

Plant to be supplied:
Steam Navvies: 2 (Wilsons's make) from Maesteg
Locos: 5 ordinary gauge from Maesteg and Port Talbot
                         1 3ft. gauge from Sec. 2 (Maesteg)
Wagons: 120 ordinary gauge (Maesteg)
                         50 3ft. gauge. (Maesteg)
1 portable steam crane. (Cardiff) Hand derricks etc.

Jack a Manning Wardle 0-4-0ST at work somewhere between Wootton Bassett and Stoke Gifford. This engine was supplied new to Pearson's in 1895 and had previously worked on their Maesteg to Port Talbot railway contract. Bearing in mind the poor weather conditions known to have been prevalent during much of the construction of the Badminton line, conditions for the footplate crew were spartan with little protection afforded by the cab. Pearson's referred to their engines as either 'straight rod' or 'tipping' type – possibly a reference to the number of coupled wheels. If this assumption is correct then *Jack* is of the tipping type.

Science Museum/Pearson Collection

Section 1 also involved a 160yd. viaduct near Somerford, the first of four brick viaducts between this point and Winterbourne.

The route through the first part of section 1 dissected a belt of yellow Oxford clay. This was a weak and potentially treacherous slime for it was found to be highly unstable when wet and so after a number of bad slips on the first cutting the slopes were trimmed to the unusually shallow angle of 5 to 1. Similarly it was impossible to utilise any of the clay for embankments and as a result the whole of the excavated material was 'run-to-spoil'. The remainder of section 1 was through the harder Oxford blue clay interspersed with patches of oolite rock. Here it was possible to vary the cutting slopes from 3 to 1 to as much as to 1 according to the stability of the rock and depth of the cutting.

No. 2 section was from 7m. 20ch. to 18m. 7ch., a distance of just under 11mls. Again the work started with the required fencing after which a temporary overland railway was laid to connect with the Malmesbury branch at Somerford. By this route the first steam navvy and the contractors steam engine *Trudy* arrived, with another engine *Bolsover* arriving shortly afterwards. As before there were also comments made about the progress of the work before winter set in and for the first time the use of horses was spoken of in relation to cutting No. 9.

At a distance of 10mls. from Wootton Bassett near to what was later to be Hullavington Station a contractors depôt and brickworks were established on land referred to locally as Kingsway Barn. This occupied an area of some 10 acres and included a brickworks as well as a museum and reading room facilities for the

A 'flying arch' bridge at 17m. 65 ch. in the cutting leading to the eastern approach to Alderton tunnel. The design of bridge was dictated by the type of strata encountered, similar conditions having given rise to the need for the same type of bridge on the former Bristol and Exeter railway between Bristol and Bridgewater.

Science Museum/Pearson Collection

workforce. This was one of three such brickworks used for supplying bricks for the contract. Large quantities of excavated material were run-to-spoil at Hullavington. *mile*

A 4m. cutting commenced west of Hullavington which later terminated in Alderton tunnel. Here the contractor had to contend with great Bathonian oolite as well as blue shale, clay, sandstone and limestone. The presence of the clay meant it was necessary to provide retaining walls at intervals throughout the cutting to prevent bulging.

Alderton tunnel was included in section 2. Work commenced here with the sinking of two access shafts 280yds. apart and a maximum of 140yds. from the ends. Digging only took place from the centre headings and rock drills were not necessary. Interestingly work on the excavation of the tunnel was only carried out during daytime and progress was estimated to be 24yds. a month. Originally the tunnel was to have been 506yds. long but for an unrecorded reason this was increased to 528yds. Alderton tunnel was situated approximately 3mls. into the 4m. excavation referred to as cutting No. 11 – hence the reason it could only be dug from the sunken headings, and it was estimated that 700,000cu.yds. of spoil would require moving. With the tunnel completed both the access shafts were filled. *what a mixture.*

Another navvy camp was sited at the west end of the Alderton tunnel site, although it would be more accurate perhaps to describe this as a shanty town, for here men and their families were housed in conditions typical of the time.

Details are also provided in the No. 2 section schedule of the amount of excavation required for each cutting. Cuttings 8 and 9 totalled 194,000cu.yds., of which 173,000cu.yds. was scheduled to be undertaken by mechanical means (steam navvy), the remainder to be cut by hand. By far the largest cutting however, but not the major engineering feature, was cutting No. 11; the work in excavating this alone was expected to take the whole of the contract time.

Around the area of cutting 12, at approximately 17mls. (later Badminton station) there is another reference to the type of ground conditions encountered including limestone. Much of this type of excavated material was later used as ballast and accounted for around three-quarters of the total requirement of 200,000cu.yds. The stability of the rock here meant the cutting sides could also be cut almost sheer.

In cutting No. 12 the phenomenon of 'Swallow Holes' was encountered. These were large subterranean chambers permanently filled with water which would then spill their contents in terrific quantities during periods of precipitation. Considerable problems were thus encountered making it impossible to keep to the anticipated timescale of work. This same rock meant bridges of a conventional type were impossible and instead recourse was made to a 'flying arch' type, itself a most graceful design.

Big though the works already referred to undoubtably were, all were easily eclipsed by section 3, Sodbury tunnel. It was a total of 2mls. in length and passed through areas of Forest marble at its east end, changing to lower lias at the western end. Further 'Swallow Holes' were also encountered requiring a 3ft. culvert to be laid beneath rail level which was capable of discharging 7 million gallons of water in 24 hours. Both Pearson's and the GWR were confident that this was more than sufficient to deal with anything nature could provide.

but we are not so confident!

The west end of Sodbury tunnel in September 1900. Excavation for the tunnel was undertaken outwards from seven shafts as it was not possible to dig in from either end. Here shoring has been added to the face as the cutting is excavated prior to the provision of a front portal.

Science Museum/Pearson Collection

Work on the tunnel – which was to be brick-lined throughout, was estimated to occupy 2 years and although the date of commencement is not recorded it would have been likely to be soon after the start of the contract. Tunnelling began with the sinking of the access shafts (it was not possible to dig from either end at first as the approach cuttings were then incomplete). There were seven access shafts the deepest of which was recorded as 279ft. Each was 12ft. in diameter and besides allowing for access to the workings six were later retained to provide ventilation for the tunnel. Above each shaft stationary engines and winding gear were situated, the circular cutting of the shafts meaning that timber shoring was not required until a depth of 80ft. was reached.

Once at the bottom both sides were worked concurrently from 25ft. wide headings. Certain sections also had a small 'bottom-heading' connecting them, although it is not clear if this applied to the complete length of the working. Work was programmed on the basis of thirteen shifts per week – 6 days and seven nights with the intention that

Inside Sodbury tunnel 28.1.1902. The men are positioned underneath No. 3 access shaft which can be seen as the opening in the tunnel roof. Notice also the curved side walls of the actual tunnel. Access to the workings was via a bucket suspended from a derrick above each access shaft and in this way men, animals, bricks and equipment were lowered to the working. The same route was taken for the removal of excavated material. It is known that on at least one occasion the Directors of the GWR descended in a bucket to view the progress of the workings.

Science Museum/Pearson Collection

within six months all the access shafts would be complete leaving two years for the actual horizontal tunnelling. The extra three months were timetabled 'as security . . . for lack of miners or bricks . . .'. From the access way the excavations were undertaken on a 'see-saw' pattern, with one being mined whilst the other was lined with brick. The rate of progress here was set at five yards of headway per week with seven shifts required for lining.

At the west end of Sodbury tunnel there was a further brickworks capable of turning out 100,000 bricks per week. The bricks themselves were dried in the open and burnt in open kilns before an inclined pulley system (1 in 2½), with overhead ropes transported the bricks to the top of the access shafts ready for distribution. The pulley system could accommodate 50 x 20 ton loads daily. Nearby at Chipping Sodbury station were the offices of Mr W.W. Grierson, the GWR resident engineer. He was assisted by Messrs Brown, Maynard and Scott. With the tunnel completed the six shafts retained for ventilation were surmounted by ornamental towers 35ft. high each of which stood on a mound of material excavated from the workings.

Excavation at No. 4 shaft, eastwards, Sodbury tunnel, 28.1.1902. Work is taking place on excavating the headings and an amount of shoring can be seen. Notice the bricks awaiting use as the lining, it is also very noticeable just what little protection is afforded to the men in the event of falls. The photograph is recorded as having been taken by 'magnesium flashlight'.

Science Museum/Pearson Collection

The stone from cutting No. 12 was also brought to the Sodbury site where a ballast grinding machine referred to as 'Perforated Pan' was in use from July 1898. A similar machine and again with that nickname was also in use at the Old Sodbury brickworks from about the same time.

Section 4 took the work from the west end of Sodbury tunnel at 20m. 45ch. to 25m. 43ch. and included just under 2mls of branch line to connect with the new line at what would later become the Westerleigh junctions with the Midland Railway at Yate. West of the tunnel and Chipping Sodbury station was one of the few sections (¼m.) of level railway compared with the ruling 1 in 300 gradient on either side. It was included so that water troughs could be added later. Contemporary records refer to Pearson's

Could an agreement not be reached to decide which abbreviation should be used?

The west end of Sodbury tunnel with Old Sodbury village above the portal. Notice the temporary contractor's track and crossover together with the pile of bricks on what was later the down line.
Railway Magazine

having established the offices of their resident engineer at the site of what was later Chipping Sodbury station. There is no record however of any other major office or contractors depôt at this point.

At a distance of 22mls. from the start was the Lillyput Quarry from which large amounts of stone were taken. As the quarry was hard by the south of the new line direct access was possible whilst the public road from Doddington to Chipping Sodbury also passed nearby.

The first stage of the work for section 4 was the establishment of a temporary connection with the Midland Railway, this was again used for transporting materials to the site. Surprisingly the permanent connecting lines at Westerleigh were amongst the last works to be finished and with the gradients on this connection were to a less exacting standard compared with the main line. For much of its course on section 4 the line ran through a layer of what was described as blue clay, beneath which was either lias lime or bastard stone although small quantities of shale and marl are also referred to. Such material was first discovered during trial borings undertaken at intervals whilst there is also the reference to the clay which was later to prove so troublesome. An amount of rock was also encountered which necessitated powder blasting.

Lillyput Quarry, just east of what was later Chipping Sodbury station on the south side of the line. From here large quantities of rock were excavated to be used as ballast for the new line.

Science Museum/Pearson Collection

Trial borings

20m. 50ch.	21m. 67ch.	22m. 26ch.
Blue clay 19ft.	Blue clay 38ft.	Blue clay 8ft.
Lias lime 1ft.	Lias lime 5ft.	Bastard
Water	Stopped 25ft.	Stone 22ft.
	from bottom	

22m 50ch.	22m. 60ch.	22m. 67ch.
Blue clay 14ft.	Blue clay 14ft.	Blue clay 6ft.
Stopped by water	Black shale 10ft.	Bastard 5ft.
	White marl 6ft.	Clay 22ft.
		Lias lime 3ft.

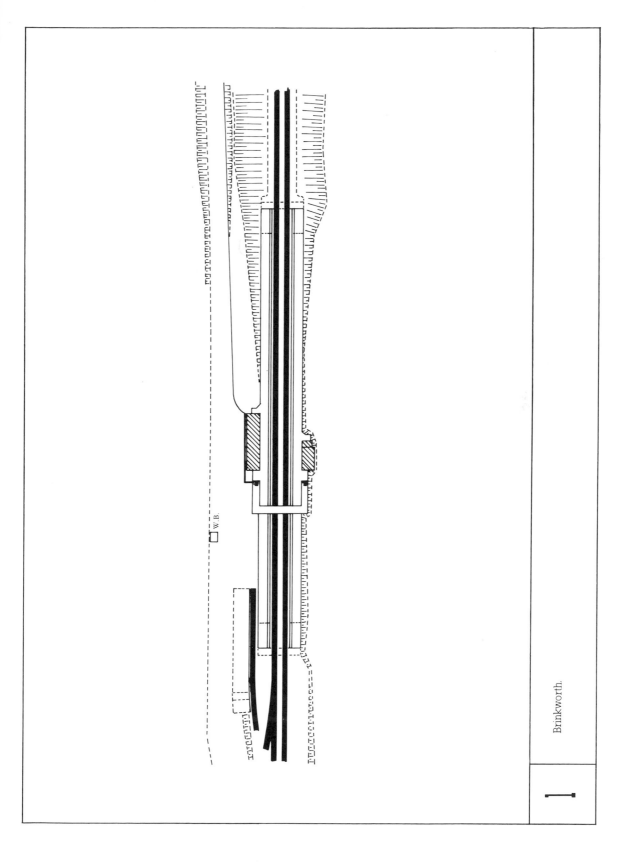

W.B.

Brinkworth.

At Wapley (west of Chipping Sodbury) Pearson's established a further large depôt to assist in the works. This occupied a 12 acre site and included a number of temporary dwelling huts, mission and reading room as well as engine and repair shops.

One particularly interesting feature of the work was the provision of a temporary wooden bridge carrying the Midland Railway from Bristol to Derby under the route. This was reputed to have cost £1000 and continued in use until the new permanent bridge was complete. Five steam navvies worked on section 4, and to begin with at least nine steam engines. The new work also involved a bridge over the existing Mineral Railway at what was later Coalpit Heath station.

The final section of the work (No. 5) was from 25m. 43ch. to the junction with the existing railway near Patchway, a distance of just over 5mls. and, as elsewhere, involving considerable work in cuttings as well as several long embankments and three viaducts. The viaducts were regarded as a priority, for it was necessary to move an estimated 675,000cu.yds of excavated material from No. 4 section over the viaduct as it was required as formation for two of the substantial embankments. Forming the embankment alone was estimated to take 18 months and with this in mind the viaduct was scheduled for completion in 15 months, i.e., by 30 April 1899 and at a rate of erection of 220cu.yds. of brickwork a week. A similar arrangement applied to the remaining two viaducts and although less material from section 4 needed to be transported across them the importance of all three is emphasised several times in contemporary records of work.

To assist in the construction of the viaducts a wooden trestle was erected on either side of the work on which a travelling gantry crane was placed so that it could run to transport material from one end to the other. Other details were conventional, with concrete bases to the brickwork piers after which timber staging was added and onto which the brick arches could be formed. In this way viaduct No. 3 was commenced first followed by No. 2 and finally No. 4.

Changes were also made to the viaduct proposals as work progressed, for at approximately 25mls. an embankment and a three-arch bridge were substituted for the eight-arch viaduct originally intended. This was due to the various underground coal workings in the area of Coalpit Heath giving rise to fears that the ground surface would be too unstable to take the weight of the supporting piers. Even so the foundations for the bridge were taken well beneath the existing coal seams.

A further brickworks was established at Stoke Gifford, and as it was capable of producing 250,000 bricks a week it may be assumed to have been the largest. Most of this production was used in erecting the viaducts on section 4.

Between the commencement of the work in 1897 and its completion in 1903 Pearson's are known to have used at least fifty steam engines. Some of these may well have been hired from the Great Western from time to time although it is known the majority were owned by the contractor. Similarly engines were transferred between sites and contracts at different times so that the engines mentioned here were not necessarily at work between Wootton Bassett and Patchway for the whole of the time from 1897 to 1903.

Standard Gauge

No.	Name	Type	Builder	Works No.	Building Date	Dates loco known to have worked
	Brancker	?	?	?	?	
	Harold	0-4-0ST	Hunslet	400	1886	
	Chesterfield	0-6-0ST	Hunslet	571	1892	1897–1902
10	*Clive*	0-6-0ST	Hunslet	573	1893	1900–1902
13	*Trudy*	0-6-0ST	Hunslet	574	1893	1900–1903
15	*Lincoln*	0-6-0ST	Hunslet	578	1893	1900–1902
	Tuxford	0-6-0ST	Hunslet	579	1893	
	Geoffrey	0-6–0ST	Hunslet	581	1893	
11	*Bolsover*	0-6-0ST	Hunslet	584	1894	1897–1903
	Spinkhill	0-6-0ST	Hunslet	585	1894	1897–1902
	Francis	0-6-0ST	Hunslet	586	1894	1897–1903
	Bernard	0-6-0ST	Hunslet	587	1893	1897–1902
22	*Woodside*	0-6-0ST	Hunslet	266	1881	1897–1902
	Annie	0-6-0ST	Hunslet	593	1893	1897–1903
	Ernest	0-6-0ST	Hunslet	594	1893	? –1903
	Aberavon	0-6-0ST	Hunslet	607	1895	1900–1903
	Garth	0-6-0ST	M/Wardle	1302	1895	
39	*Margam*	0-4-0ST	M/Wardle	1306	1895	
42	*Jack*	0-4-0ST	M/Wardle	1300	1895	
46	*Scarcliffe*	0-6-0ST	Hunslet	625	1895	
	Russia	0-6-0ST	Hunslet	626	1895	1900–1903
	Maesteg	0-4-0ST	Hunslet	627	1895	
	Dick	0-4-0ST	Hunslet	628	1895	
	Torpedo	0-4-0ST	Peckett	449	1886	
	Sam	0-4-0ST	H/Clarke	444	1895	
	Talbot	0-4-0ST	M/Wardle	1279	1895	
	Urmston	0-4-0ST	Hunslet	450	1888	
66	*Filton*	0-4-0ST	Peckett	690	1898	1897–1903
67	*George*	0-4-0ST	Peckett	729	1898	1897–1903
68	*Frank*	0-4-0ST	Peckett	730	1898	1897–1903
69	*Yate*	0-6-0ST	Peckett	718	1898	1897–1903
70	*Chipping Sodbury*	0-6-0ST	Peckett	719	1898	1897– ?
71	*Somerford*	0-6-0ST	Peckett	720	1898	1897– ?
72	*Badminton*	0-6-0ST	Peckett	721	1898	1897– ?
73	*Wootton Bassett*	0-6-0ST	Peckett	722	1898	1897–1903
74	*Patchway*	0-6-0ST	Peckett	723	1898	1897–1903
81	*The Auditor*	0-6-0ST	Chapman	1105	1895	1897– ?
	Howard	0-4-0ST	Hunslet	63	1871	1899–1902
	Corston	0-6-0ST	M/Wardle	1196	1890	
	Sully	0-4-0ST	Hunslet	367	1885	1897–1899
84	*Saltburn*	0-6-0ST	Black/Haw.	511	1883	
133		0-6-0ST	M/Wardle	595	1877	1897–1903

3ft. Gauge

No.	Name	Type	Builder	Works No.	Building Date	Dates loco known to have worked
	Huddersfield	0-4-0ST	Hunslet	74	1871	

(The practice of naming engines in association with the current contract was a regular feature of contemporary civil engineering and is displayed here to advantage.)

Stoke Gifford brickworks on the site of what was later Pugley's siding. Production here was at a maximum of 250,000 bricks per week.

Science Museum/Pearson Collection

Four thousand men were employed on the work as well as a variety of other equipment which included:

17 steam navvies of the Ruston and Proctor, Whittaker or Wilson type,
11 steam cranes,
1800 earth wagons,
75mls. of temporary track,
50,000,000 bricks,
20,000 tons of cement or lime.
The steelwork for the bridges was supplied by Alexander Findlay & Co. of Motherwell whilst the GWR provided 97lb./yd. of bull-head rail in 44ft. 6in. lengths allied to their standard rail chair. This was was laid on either Karri (West Australian) or Jarrah sleepers and set at 18 per rail length.

Sir Weetman and Lady Pearson were regular visitors to the works and whilst to the

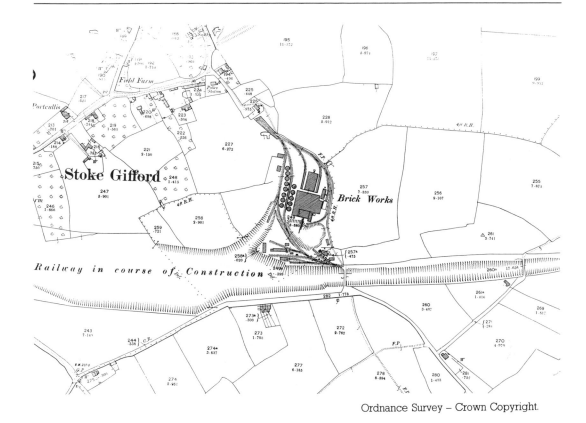

Ordnance Survey – Crown Copyright.

casual observer everything appeared to be progressing well, in reality it was a different story with the works continually behind schedule from the start and aggravated by long periods of inclement weather. In addition Oxford clay was found to be a problem on section 1 whilst similar but more severe difficulties were present on section 4. Neither of these had been found during trial borings.

Thus work progressed steadily from early 1898 and to begin with at least it appeared as if all was progressing to schedule, this despite the difficulties encountered in the workings. But nature dictated otherwise; the start and end of 1900 were exceptionally wet and consequently slips began to occur on several sections of the work, with the excavations for Sodbury tunnel being almost flooded out at the western end. The accompanying contemporary photographs graphically illustrate some of these difficulties.

A certain amount of earth slippage was to be expected on a new line, especially before the embankments and cuttings had consolidated themselves and therefore allowances were always made in the tendered cost to cover such eventualities. But conditions on the new line were nothing short of extreme and it meant that not only was the work seriously behind schedule but the contractor was forced to meet unforeseen additional costs.

Construction of viaduct No. 3. At this stage the piers have been erected and the first timber former provided. The arches would then be built around the timber which would then be removed. Notice the small steam crane and its very temporary track. Also visible are two derricks used for hauling materials to the top of the piers. Certain of the viaducts had a wooden plateway erected on either side on which ran a trestle arrangement. This was used to assist in bringing materials to the site. The plateways were removed before the line opened.

Science Museum/Pearson Collection

Despite these problems a special inspection train for the directors of the GWR to view progress on the new line was arranged for Tuesday 16 July 1901. It may be assumed that the original starting point and destination was Paddington although records record only part of the timings:

Depart Swindon	10.55	– worked by contractor's
Arrive Wootton Bassett	11.03	engine from Wootton
Depart Wootton Bassett	11.13	Bassett to Sodbury
Somerford	11.55	East. Thence on foot

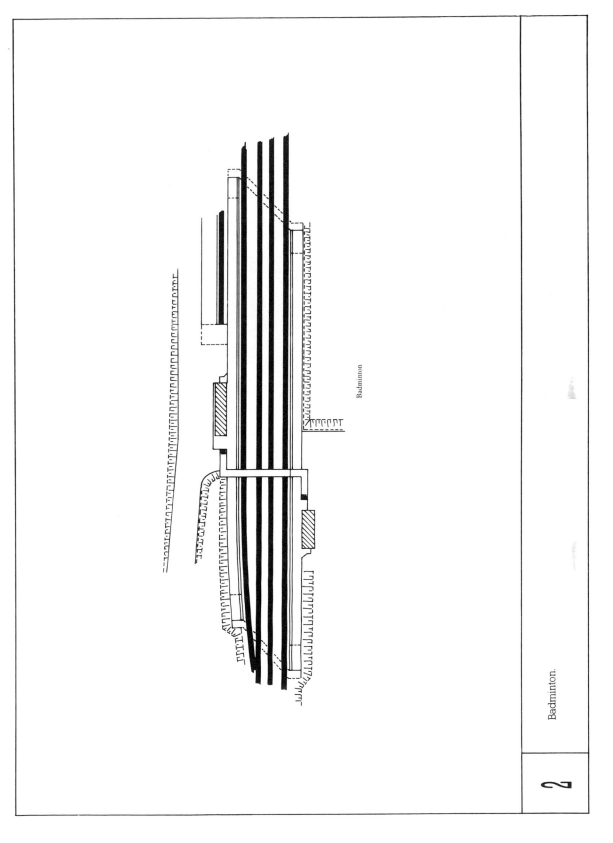

Badminton

Contractor's staff at the Sodbury tunnel site in September 1900.

N. L. Diamond

Sodbury East	12.50	to Cross Hands for
Arrive Cross Hands	1.15	luncheon. Resuming
Depart Cross Hands	2.00	loco haulage again
Sodbury tunnel (west end)	2.15	with contractor's
Arrive Filton	4.15	engine from Sodbury
Depart Filton	4.20	Tunnel – west end
Arrive Bristol	4.30	to Filton.

The directors were thus able to view at first hand the difficulties being experienced and particularly the latest problems which were slips on the embankments of section 4, principally affecting a half-mile section west from about 25mls. near to what was later Coalpit Heath station.

Perhaps satisfied by what they had seen, the signal engineer placed his order for the signalling equipment for the new line on 25.7.1901; it included the following signalbox nameplates:

BRINKWORTH SIGNALBOX
LITTLE SOMERFORD SIGNALBOX
HULLAVINGTON SIGNALBOX

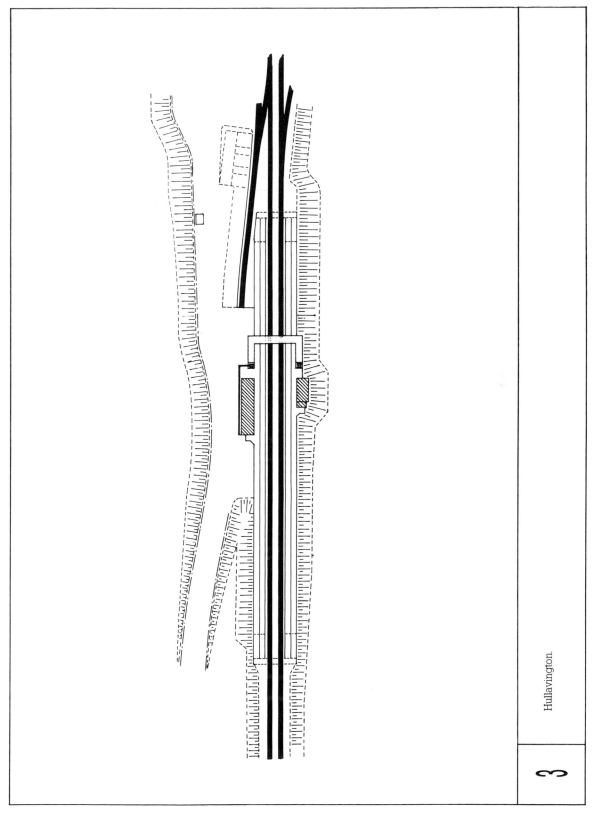

Hullavington.

3

Slip on No. 4 section, 9.2.1900. The view is looking at the south side of the embankment leading to Winterbourne viaduct and clearly shows not only the height of the embankment but the difficulties which were encountered.

Science Museum/Pearson Collection

BADMINTON SIGNALBOX
SODBURY SIGNALBOX
COAL PIT HEATH SIGNALBOX*
WINTERBOURNE SIGNALBOX
STOKE GIFFORD EAST SIGNALBOX
STOKE GIFFORD WEST SIGNALBOX

* Some confusion occurs in the early references to this location as to the spelling of the name. It is generally accepted that 'Coalpit' is one word although the GWR had evidently not decided as such at the time the nameplate order was placed.

But despite this obvious step towards final completion progress on the civil engineering for the new line was already drastically behind schedule. So much so that a graph of the period shows the best performance to have been 45% in arrears with the worst effort an amazing 383% behind schedule.

Initially to assist in countering the additional costs Pearson's requested that the

Again on the same section and difficulties this time with a cutting after subsidence in the summer of 1900. The five men visible are unlikely to have had much impact in putting right this problem by themselves.

Science Museum/Pearson Collection

GWR supplement the regular monthly amount (believed to have been £30,000) paid to them by the GWR under the contract and this was agreed, a further £50,000 being paid on 11.9.1901. However, in July 1902 Pearson's found it necessary to submit a number of extra claims to compensate for the additional work. These totalled £252,479, just over 25% extra on top of the original cost of the tender. Not surprisingly the GWR rejected this out of hand and following an increasing series of acrimonious exchanges between the two concerns the matter was sent to arbitration under the chairmanship of Sir Benjamin Baker.

The dispute between Pearson's and the GWR was to drag on for several years. The contractor's case was based on the fact that after five years of hard work on forty different faces they were £312,000 out of pocket, or as much as £457,000 if loss of profits was also taken into consideration. They contended that the work had proven to be a 'wet' contract and their original estimate had been based on a 'dry' line. The

A dramatic view of a works train in the flooded Sodbury cutting in November 1899. The view is interesting in several respects not least of which is that the engine is probably a Peckett-type owned by the contractor. Notice also the temporary water tower on the top of the far cutting – a number of these were placed at intervals throughout the line as water supply for the contractors engines etc drawing their supply from wells the quality of which was often suspect. Its use on this occassion must be considered superfluous!

Science Museum/Pearson Collection

GWR countered this with the argument that the work had been completed in nothing short of a magnificent way, but they could not bear any responsibility for errors made in surveys or original estimates by the contractor.

Having listened to both sides of the argument Baker awarded a further £147,400 to Pearson's. However, this they considered to be insufficient and appealed to the House of Lords. The appeal was eventually heard on 29 October 1907 but was unsuccessful and costs were awarded against the firm. Such an unfortunate result would almost certainly have bankrupted a smaller concern, but Pearson's were made of sterner stuff and the only notable outcome was a resolution never again to tender for work for the GWR, which they never did.

The railway complete and ready for traffic. This is bridge No. 1 on the new line (No. 220 from Paddington). Excluding culverts there were approximately 100 bridges on the new line between Wootton Bassett and Stoke Gifford.

Science Museum/Pearson Collection

We have jumped ahead in time again and must return to 1902 when the work was at last approaching its conclusion and the railway nearly ready for opening. A minor prelude to this had been a decision by the GWR to alter the name of the existing Somerford station on the Malmesbury branch and so on 22.12.1902 an official notice to this effect was sent out from Paddington.

Legally no new railway could be opened for passenger traffic until a satisfactory inspection had been completed by the Board of Trade, although there was nothing to stop goods traffic being worked without seeking such authority. Consequently the line was opened by the GWR for the use of goods from Wootton Bassett as far as Badminton on 1.1.1903 with one goods train daily each way between Swindon and Badminton. Five months later on 1.5.1903 the line was opened for goods throughout. Both can be considered as a two-fold move for the movement of trains, albeit at restricted speeds, would assist in consolidating the earthworks whilst at the same time the GWR could begin to gain some benefit from what was an expensive new addition to their railway infrastructure. Strangely enough there is no reference to an inspection of the new junctions for the line at either end of the route and as these were already used by passenger trains they would certainly have required approval.

Thus on 14.3.1903 a letter was sent by the then GWR General Manager, Sir Joseph Wilkinson to the Board of Trade advising them that it was intended to open the line for passengers on 1.7.1903. (The GWR had originally hoped to open the line to passengers on 1.4.1903 but its incomplete state obviously precluded this.) Unusually no reply was received and so a second approach was made on 18.5.1903. Subsequently on 26 June Col. H.A. Yorke visited the new route. As ever this worthy individual produced a superbly detailed report containing much useful information and it is herewith reproduced in full – complete with contemporary spellings etc:

> I have the honour to report for the information of the Board of Trade, that in compliance with the instructions contained in your Minute of the 8th. inst. I have inspected the Bristol and South Wales Direct Ry, belonging to the Great Western Ry Company, being railways Nos. 1 & 3 of the Company's Act of 1896.
>
> The line commences by a double junction with the G.Western main line a short distance west of Wootton Bassett station and terminates by a double junction with the main lines to S.Wales via Severn Tunnel at Patchway Station. There is also a short loop line 74.5 chains long from Stoke Gifford to Filton, being No.4. of 1896 which I also inspected. Railways Nos.1 & 3 have a total length of 29 miles 59.75 chains, and are double throughout, except at four stations, viz Little Somerford, Badminton, Chipping Sodbury and Coalpit Heath, and also at Stoke Gifford marshalling depot where there are four lines.
>
> Details of construction are given in the statement forwarded by the Co. with their letter dated 18th May 1903 (R5807) and need not be repeated here. The line has been so constructed as to obtain very favourable gradients, which, with the exception of a length at the commencement of the line having an inclination of 1 in 237, are nowhere worse than 1 in 300. Similarly the curvature is easy, the sharpest curves having radii of 40 chains, which only occur at the two ends of the line, whilst the remaining curves have radii of not less than a mile. It is not surprising to find, that on a line so carefully laid out as to gradients and curves, the earthworks are very heavy. The deepest cutting has a maximum depth of 72ft. and the highest embankment a height of 69ft.
>
> The cuttings seem to be standing fairly well, but two of the embankments, viz those known as No. 3 bank, and the Winterbourne bank, have given a good deal of trouble, owing to slips. Counterparts and drains of steel or copper slag have been and are being, constructed in the worst places, and buttresses of the same material are also being employed where possible. These measures are having a beneficial effect but the banks do not yet appear to have attained a position of stability, nor is this likely to be the case for some time to come. Great caution will therfor have to be exercised for the safety of trains passing over these embankments. Watchmen supplied with flags, detonators, and the necessary appliances should constantly patrol the embankments referred to, and the speed of trains passing over these portions of the line, viz No. 3 bank and Winterbourne bank, should not for the present exceed 15 miles an hour.
>
> There are 82 bridges (viz 43 over the line, and 39 under the line), 4 viaducts (with 32 openings), 2 tunnels (one 2 miles long), and 33 culverts upon the railway. I carefully examined all these works, and found no indications whatever of weakness or failure in

Somerford viaduct from the south which consisted of thirteen arches one of which carries the River Avon underneath. The view was taken when the structure had just been completed, its construction being in what appears to be a light coloured brick. This is deceptive, however, as the actual brick colour is much darker in practice and more akin to an 'engineers blue'.

Science Museum/Pearson Collection

Coalpit Heath.

4

any one of them, and the workmanship appeared to be uniformly good. It it not possible for me to submit the plans of all these works to a searching examination, but I am satisfied that the design and constructions are not such as to transgress these rules and precautions which practice and experience have proved to be necessary for safety.

The girders under the line seem to have sufficient strength, and gave very moderate and uniform deflections, when tested in the usual manner by heavy engines.

There are seven stations on the new line, viz Brinkworth, Little Somerford, Hullavington, Badminton, Chipping Sodbury, Coalpit Heath, Winterbourne, all of which have up and down platforms 400ft. long and 3ft. high. Four of these stations have as already stated 4 lines through them, viz two platform lines, and two through lines; the remaining stations have two lines only. Good waiting accommodation, including ladies rooms and lavatories, and conveniences for men, is provided at each place. There is a footbridge at each station to connect the two platforms; clocks and name-board have been fixed; and the arrangements are satisfactory; alterations are in progress at Filton Station on the main line, but these were not ready for inspection. Wootton Bassett station also on the main line, has been rebuilt and contains full accommodation of all descriptions, besides a footbridge to connect the up and down platforms.

I inspected the following signalboxes,

Brinkworth station 'box	16 levers in use	5 spare
Little Somerford	48	13
Hullavington	30	9
Badminton	48	13
Chipping Sodbury	48	13
Westerleigh East	18	5
Westerleigh West	15	8
Coalpit Heath station	31	0
Coalpit Heath G/Frame⋆	4	0
Winterbourne	23	4

⋆ locked from the signalbox.

Stoke Gifford East 'box	20	11
Stoke Gifford West	34	11
Patchway station	38	7
Filton	38	7
Wootton Bassett East	46	11
Wootton Bassett West	31	6

The interlocking in all cases was correct and the only matters in connection with the signalling which requires attention are the advanced starting signal at Brinkworth requires to be raised so as to give it a better background; catch points require to be inserted in the junction lines connecting the S. Wales direct railway with the Midland Ry at Westerleigh East 'Box. The junction lines are not completed, and were not submitted for inspection (see note at end of chapter) the points and signals require to be connected up with the levers operating them at Coalpit Heath Station.

In addition to the above I notice that short lengths of handrailing are required above the wingwalls of some of the wooden bridges, to protect the risk of platelayers and others who may be walking alonside the line in the execution of their duty from falling into the roadways below, also that a notice board warning pedestrians to 'beware of trains' should be erected at the footpath crossing near Brinkworth.

The railway as a general rule is in excellent order, and the permanent way is of the highest standard. But I do not consider that any new railway should be run over at high speed when first opened, as it is necessary for safety that the 'way' should be thoroughly consolidated before a speed of anything like 60 miles an hour or more is attempted. I therefore consider that for the present the maximum speed should not anywhere exceed 35 miles an hour, except over No 3 bank and Winterbourne bank, where it should not exceed 15 miles an hour. These speeds should be absolute in the former case for 1 month, and in the latter for 3 months, and at the expiration of these periods, it may be left to the enquiries of the Company in charge of the line to decide, whether any, and if so what, increase of speed may be safely permitted.

Subject to the above conditions, I can recommend the Board of Trade authorise the use of the new line (Rys Nos. 1, 3 & 4 of 1896) for passenger traffic.

I have the honour to be your obedient servant

H.A. Yorke

P.S. Major Dymott kindly accompanied me and assisted me with this inspection. His help was of much advantage, as it enabled me to complete the inspection in two days; otherwise it would have occupied three days at least. – H.A.Y.

Despite the short time remaining to the intended opening date passenger services commenced as intended and on 1 July 1903 the public service was inaugurated apparently without ceremony of any sort, although the children at most of the schools along the route were given a day's holiday.

Shortly afterwards on 17 July 1908, Sir James Inglis the new GWR General Manager (Inglis had replaced Wilkinson in the post as G.M. in June 1903) wrote to the Board of Trade concerning the previously advised overall speed limit;

Sir,

According to the letter of the Board of Trade of the 29th. ultimo, covering a copy of the Report made by Colonel Yorke of his insepction of the new Bristol and South Wales Direct Railway, it will be remembered that the approval of the Board of Trade to the opening of that line for passenger traffic was made conditional upon a restriction of speed to 15 miles an hour in the case of two specified sections, and to 35 miles over all.

I now beg to submit, however, that the experience which has been gained of the running of passenger trains over the new line since the 1st. instant, and the much longer experience in connection with the running of goods trains, justifies the Company in suggesting that, except at the two particular places specified in Colonel Yorke's Report (where it is not suggested that the present speed of 15 miles per hour should at present be exceeded) normal running may now be sanctioned.

In making this representation to the Board of Trade I am not only giving expression to my own opinion, based as it is upon an intimate aquaintance with all the conditions affecting the construction of the line supplemented by the experience gained since it was opened for goods traffic partly on the 1st. January, and wholly on the 1st. May last, but I am supported by the views of the Resident Engineer and of our Locomotive people.

I hope therfore that the Board of Trade will experience no difficulty in referring the requirement in question to Colonel Yorke for review and that the Company may hope to hear that with the exception already alluded to normal speed may now be observed by passenger trains working over the new line.

It need scarcely be added that every precaution to ensure safe working will be taken.

I am, Sir,

Your obedient Servant,

James Inglis

Rodbourne Lane bridge at 9m.0ch. which carried the former Chippenham to Malmesbury road beneath the railway. The arches were on a slight 3in. skew to the horizontal and provided for a maximum headway of 31ft. above road level via a span of 24ft. 9in.

Science Museum/Pearson Collection

Unfortunately no record of a reply appears to have survived, although it is known that on 16.10.1903 a further letter was sent by the GWR advising that all the requests mentioned in the previous inspection had been carried out. Possibly this was also the time that the 15 m.p.h. speed restriction was relaxed although it is not clear from the records.

Bridge No. 282 this time carrying a private road over the railway to Sergeant's Farm. In the background is the Westerleigh East curve and the bracket signal for the junction can just be seen through the bridge. Under an eye-glass it is also just possible to discern the original Westerleigh East signalbox in the 'V' of the junction leading to the Midland lines.

Science Museum/Pearson Collection

Bearing in mind the magnitude of the work involved, seven years was probably not an unrealistic timescale from the passing of the original Act to the eventual opening of the new railway. Now though the question to be asked would be – 'Was it still needed to fulfill the originally intended role?' – time would indeed tell.

Note; The matter of the junctions at Westerleigh and the corresponding connection with the MR at Yate was a matter of some debate between the GWR and MR at this time. From the inspection it would appear as if these lines were basically complete in 1903 and were probably worked over by freight traffic shortly afterwards. A dispute arose, however, with the MR over through running between the new lines and the joint Severn & Wye route the consequence of which was that the connection was closed in February 1907. It was re-opened in March 1908 although Board of Trade inspection to allow for passenger working did not take place until late 1908. At the same time relevant signalboxes were also affected with periods of closure. The matter is discussed at length in Chapter 4.

Local stone has been used for bridge No. 283 on the west curve at Westerleigh on what is now a busy thoroughfare. The first bridge carries the main line from Chipping Sodbury (right) to Coalpit Heath (left) with the MR connection behind.

Science Museum/Pearson Collection

The eleven arches of Winterbourne viaduct complete (sometimes known as Hackford viaduct) and awaiting the first trains. The colour of the bricks is again deceptively light.

Science Museum/Pearson Collection

Private and not for Publication.

GREAT WESTERN RAILWAY.

Circular No. 1914.

GENERAL MANAGER'S OFFICE,
PADDINGTON STATION,
LONDON, W.
22nd December, 1902.

SOMERFORD STATION: ALTERATION OF NAME.

It is decided to alter the name of Somerford Station, on the Dauntsey and Malmesbury Branch of the Railways of the Company, to

GREAT SOMERFORD,

the alteration to take effect from the 1st January, 1903.

On and from the date named, all letters, invoices, way-bills and truck labels emanating from or intended for this Station must be addressed "Great Somerford."

This alteration has become necessary through the construction of a second station at Somerford on the new South Wales and Bristol Direct Railway, which will be known as "Little Somerford."

Please acknowledge receipt to the Head of your Department.

L. WILKINSON,

General Manager.

THREE

AN EDWARDIAN ACHIEVEMENT – THE STATIONS

I can safely say that it will rank amongst the very highest class of modern marvels of railway construction in this country of wonderful railway work in general

A contributor to the 'Railway Magazine', 1902

WOOTTON BASSETT

As has already been referred to briefly, Wootton Bassett station had existed for some 60 years before the opening of the new line. However, the coming of the South Wales direct railway prompted a rebuilding of the facilties in a far more commodious style.

The station served the small Wiltshire town of the same name, a town which could hardly be expected to support a station in its own right for it boasted a population of less than four thousand. Apart from its importance as a railway junction, Wootton Bassett is known for its half-timbered town hall and the church of St Bartholemew, the latter sporting a wall-painting which depicts the murder of Thomas à Becket.

Before describing the new rail facilities in detail it is perhaps appropriate to return to the earlier days at which time it was just a stopping place boasting only up and down platforms, each surmounted by one of Brunel's 'chalet style' station buildings erected in local stone. A small goods yard was also provided on the up side of the line and just west of the passenger station. Here there was a goods shed and also a headshunt leading to a loading dock. On the opposite side of the track was a single trailing siding, the up and down lines connected by a trailing crossover again at the west end of the station.

Around 1873 a ten-lever signalbox was erected to control the layout. This was increased to eighteen levers at the end of 1887, by which time a number of changes concerning the sidings and points had been made to the basic facilities. Mixed gauge track was used on the main lines and crossover although the sidings were only laid to the narrow gauge. Surprisingly the signalbox did not carry a location nameplate until early 1899 when on 18.1.1899 a casting of WOOTTON BASSETT SIGNALBOX was ordered from Reading signal works.

The new Wootton Bassett station looking west shortly before the opening of the South Wales line. The buildings were constructed by the firm of Eli Hadley & Sons, who also provided the cover to the footbridge, although the main structure was from standard GWR fittings. In the distance the timber East signalbox can be seen, the 'Xs' on the signals to the South Wales line indicating that these were not yet in use. Under a glass a number of the items on the inventory are visible including seats and barrows. What appears to be an outside-framed saddle tank is shunting in the up side yard. Notice the platform surface, much of which was gravel – this was paved in later years. The small wooden building on the up platform nearest the camera is a two-lever ground cabin used in connection with shunting in and out of the down refuge siding which was behind the camera. Inside, a bell was used for communication with the East signalbox. Although the hut was provided as the crossover it was at that time too far away to be worked by conventional mechanical means.

British Railways

With the connection for the new line destined to be just west of the station the GWR took the opportunity to rebuild the station and accordingly in early 1901 tenders were invited for the work. Whether Pearson's did not in fact tender or if they were unsuccessful is unclear for on 1.4.1901, Eli. Hadley & Sons of Old Hill, Stafford were awarded the work, their tender of £4,409 16s. 4d. having been accepted.

Hadley's were only involved in the erection of the new buildings and other fixed structures, the GWR themselves had already commenced work on a various changes to the track layout.

Besides the new station the contractor was also to demolish the existing facilities as well as provide a temporary station. Details of this are given in the work schedule and included, '. . . a temporary timber building about 26ft. by 10ft. on plan and 10ft. high, comprising clerks office, 8ft. long with desk and ticket window; booking office, 10ft. long; ladies' room, 8ft. long with WC in same . . . the roof to be covered with felt . . . alcove or waiting shelter on down side, 10ft. by 8ft. in the clear with a 4ft. opening in front, with all necessary windows, and with seats at back and sides, and lighting, etc, as required.'

From the opposite side and a number of the staff can be seen posed for the camera. The view is taken from a 'Wrench' series coloured postcard dated 1919. Notice the up starting signal situated against the Marlborough Road bridge and yet on the down side of the line – this was to afford better sighting on what was a left hand curve although not visible as such from the angle of the photograph.

Author's Collection

The complete work was costed as follows:

	£	s.	d.
Preliminaries and contingencies	241	10	0
Temporary works and demolition	119	9	2
Station buildings, up side	640	1	1
Ditto, down side	398	10	10
Platform coverings, up side	464	4	7
Ditto, down side	547	9	3
Drainage to station buildings etc	66	4	2
Internal plumbing to ditto	130	19	3
Platform walls and pavings	615	3	7
Covering to footbridge	125	17	6
Lock-up	212	11	8
Horse and carriage landing	378	15	4
Cattle pens	267	0	5
Lighting	146	9	5
Maintenance for six months	15	0	0
	4,369	6	4
Include 1 percent for Surveyor's fees	65	10	0
	4,434	16	4
Credit value of materials resulting from demolition	25	0	0
Amount of Tender	£4,409	16	4

Twelve months were allowed for completion within which a condition stated that no work was to be carried out on a Sunday.

Whilst the new station was under construction the GWR were engaged on modifications to the track layout. A double junction was provided for the South Wales line with holding loops to either side. On the original Bristol line a down loop 1,665ft. long was laid west of the station, and an up refuge siding able to hold 50 wagons stood parallel with the up Bristol line. A similar down refuge siding, this time able to hold 65 wagons was provided east of the roadbridge and at the opposite end of the station. Special instructions and bell signals applied to shunting into this siding, part of which was controlled from a small ground cabin located on the up platform. Within the yard were cattle pens, a goods shed fronting a 50ft. loading platform and a 172ft. loading ramp. There was also a 1-ton yard crane outside the goods shed and a private weighbridge.

Controlling the station were two signalboxes, Wootton Bassett East and West. The East 'box was brought into use on 13.7.1902 at which time the original brick 'box was closed. The new 'box measured 38ft. x 13ft. x 10ft. – to the operating floor. Wootton

Another contemporary coloured card and this time from the 'Valentine' series. The view is of the up side station approach looking towards the goods yard with the goods shed just discernable in the distance. Immediately through the gates on the right is the privately owned cart weighbridge which could record up to 8 tons on a plate 10ft. x 7ft..

Author's Collection

Bassett West had been brought into use a little earlier on 17.11.1901 and was slightly smaller at 29ft. x 12ft. x 11ft. Both contained lever frames with double twist locking and at 5in. centres. The appropriate cast nameplates for the new boxes were ordered on 12.5.1901.

Access to the station for both passenger and vehicles was from the Marlborough Road which crossed the railway by a brick overbridge at the east end. Alongside the 'up' side the approach continued on to the goods yard whilst opposite the 'up' side approach and facing the station entrance was the Beaufort Hotel. The new station boasted all the usual facilities and was contained within a pleasing mellow brick structure under a gently sloping roof.

Being in a prime agricultural area there was a considerable amount of goods traffic handled, including coal, fertilizer, grain, cake and livestock – figures for the actual traffic handled along with the other stations on the new line are given in Appendix B. Timber was another important traffic and a large open air stacking ground was provided at the Bristol end of the station on the down side.

In charge of the station was a station master, who originally oversaw some twenty other employees, a figure which included ten signalmen as not only were the men at the station 'boxes counted in the total, but also those at the neighbouring 'boxes of Studley and Wootton Bassett incline – east and west of the station, respectively, on the

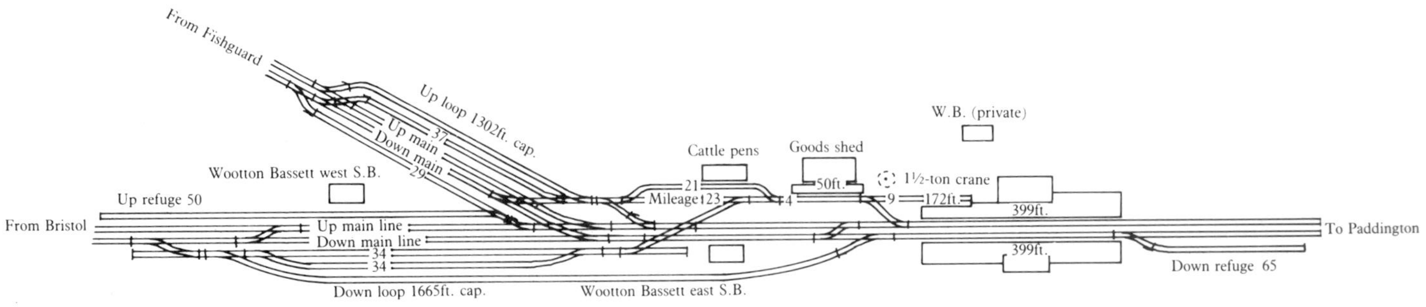

From Fishguard

Up loop 1302ft. cap.

37

Up main

Down main

29

Wootton Bassett west S.B.

Up refuge 50

From Bristol

Up main line

Down main line

34

34

Down loop 1665ft. cap.

Wootton Bassett east S.B.

Mileage 123

21

Cattle pens

Goods shed

50ft.

1½-ton crane

9

172ft.

W. B. (private)

399ft.

399ft.

Down refuge 65

To Paddington

Wootton Bassett.

5

No.4951 *Penteford Hall* at the head of down empty stock for the Badminton line at Wootton Bassett, 18.9.1955. On the left is the small goods lock-up whilst the former timber stacking foreground had formally occupied the space between the down line and the Bristol goods siding on the right.

R.C. Riley

original Bristol main line. The remaining ten staff were subdivided as follows; 2 general clerks, 2 goods shunters, 3 porters, 1 goods checker, 1 vanman. Grades as well as staff duties are known to have varied over the years. An interesting comment is found in a staff review feasibility study for 1947 which states: 'The station is a main line junction and in the event of a temporary absence of the station master, there is no one at present except a grade 1 porter to assume any executive responsibility. In this connection it may be mentioned that the present station master has not taken his weekly half-holiday for about six years.'

A fascinating item in the records is an inventory of the furniture and effects at the station including their values as they existed in August 1905. It is reproduced here in full:

Down Platform Waiting Room

	£	s.	d.
1 Seat, oak. No. 148	6	10	0
1 Table, oak. 5ft. x 3ft.	4	10	0
2 No. 4 stained boards	1	13	8
1 Fender, curb		5	0
1 Smoking notice		2	6

Ladies Waiting Room

1 Table, oak. 4ft. x 2ft.	2	15	0
1 Seat, No. 48 5ft.	2	10	0
1 Chair, No. 72	1	5	9
1 Fender, curb		5	0
1 Linoleum 11ft. x 9ft.		11	0
1 Linoleum 10ft. x 5ft.		3	4

Down Platform

2 Forms, No. 50 10ft.	1	10	0
4 Fire buckets		10	0
2 Seats, iron legs 10ft.	1	15	0
9 No. 4 boards	6	10	6
1 No. 7 board	1	4	0
1 No. 9 board	1	12	0
1 Trolley No.42. 12in. i.r. tyred	4	17	3
1 Trolley No.42. 12in. iron tyred	3	4	0

Up Platform Ladies Waiting Room

1 Table, oak 3ft. 6in. x 2ft	2	10	0
1 Seat No. 48 8ft.	4	0	0
1 Chair No. 72	1	5	9
1 Frame of views		15	0
1 Linoleum 12ft. x 10ft.		13	4
1 Linoleum 12ft. x 3ft.		4	0

Waiting Room

1 Table, oak 4ft. x 2ft. 6in.	3	10	0
1 Seat, No. 48	4	0	0
2 No. 4 boards, stained	1	13	8
1 No. 3 board, stained		17	9
1 Fare list frame. 5 sheet	1	14	9
1 Fender		5	0
1 Smoking notice		2	6

Booking Office

1 Desk & counter 12ft. 6in. x 2ft. 6in. with oak top, cupboards, drawers and book rack.	12	10	0
1 Book rack, 3ft. x 2ft. x 1ft.	1	0	0
1 Ticket stamp		15	0
2 Book racks 24in. x 20in. x 14in.	1	10	0
1 Set pigeon holes 3ft.x2ft.x13in.	1	0	0
1 Desk, 4ft. x 2ft. 6in.		7	6
1 Chair, No. 72	1	5	9
1 Stool, No. 26		15	6
1 Telephone	3	0	0

1 Stationary case, tin		1	6
1 Letter rack		1	6
1 water well		2	6
1 Fender		5	0
1 Cash, safe, iron	7	10	0
1 Ticket issuing case, 264 tubes	9	15	0
2 Blinds		15	0
1 Stock ticket case, 6 drawers	3	8	0
1 Copying press, 22in. x 14in.	4	0	0

Parcels Office

1 Parcel rack, 8ft. x 6ft.	1	10	0
1 Stool. No. 26		12	0
1 Fender		5	0
1 Label rack, 36 holes		16	9
1 Label rack, 27 holes		12	0
1 Side counter 5ft.6in. x 3ft.6in. with cupboards and book racks, also 1 weighing machine. GWR No.744 capacity 5 cwt. by H. Pooley	2	0	0
2 Blinds		15	0
1 Ambulance stretcher	2	0	0
5 Hand lamps		12	6
2 Brooms, hair sweeping		6	0
1 Bass broom		2	9
1 Flap counter 4ft.6in. x 2ft.6in. with cupboards and drawers		15	0

Station Masters Office

1 Table No. 82	8	8	0
2 Chairs No. 72	2	11	6
1 Basket, waste paper, wire		1	6
1 Ambulance box	1	11	0
1 Book rack, corres. rack, & Cupboard 15ft. x 2ft.9in. x 11in.	2	0	0
1 Book rack 2ft.3in. x 21in. x 12in.		10	0
1 Fender		5	0
1 Hat & coat rack		2	6
1 Stationary case, tin		1	6
1 Box, tin, gratuitous		1	6
1 Coal scuttle		2	6

Up Platform

4 Fire buckets		10	0
1 Mop		1	9
1 Can, watering		2	6

2 No. 7 boards	2	8	0
1 No. 9 board	1	12	0
3 No. 4 boards	2	3	6
4 No. 3 boards	3	1	0
1 Special board		7	6
2 Seats, iron legs	1	15	0
1 Form, No. 50 10ft. long		13	4
1 Pair of steps, 9 treads		12	0
1 Trolley No.42 12in. i.r.tyres	4	17	0
1 Trolley No.42 12" solid	3	4	0
1 Luggage barrow (damaged)		7	6
1 Sack truck No.2	1	0	0
1 Clock	2	10	0

Goods Locker Shed

1 Side shelf 4ft. 6in. x 18in.		2	0
2 Fire buckets		5	0
1 Hand lamp		2	6
1 Stove	1	0	0
1 Sack truck No. 2	1	0	0
1 Traverser weighing machine GWR No. 743 capacity 22 cwt.	Not priced		

East Signalbox

1 Cupboard 5ft. x 3ft.6in. x 12in.	1	5	0
1 Desk 3ft.x 5ft.6in. x 18in.		18	0
1 Table 3ft. x 20in. x 2ft.6in. high		5	0
1 Cupboard & desk 5ft.6in. x 2ft. x 1ft.		15	0
1 Stool 3ft.		4	0
1 Chair, Windsor		2	6
1 Stove, coal	2	5	0
1 Coal scuttle		2	6
1 Bucket		2	6
1 Clock		10	0
3 Telephones	9	0	0
1 Mat 3ft. x 2ft.		2	0

West Signalbox

1 Cupboard 5ft.6in. x 1ft.	1	5	0
1 Desk 3ft. x 3ft.6in. x 18in.		18	0
1 Table 3ft. x 20in. x 2ft.6in.		5	0
2 Telephones	6	0	0
1 Cupboard & desk 3ft.6in. x 2ft. x 1ft.		15	0
1 Fender		5	0
1 Clock	1	10	0
1 Poker			6

1 Cinder lifter			6
2 Buckets		5	0
1 Coal scuttle		2	6
1 Stool 3ft.		3	0
1 Mat 3ft. x 2ft.		2	0
1 Oil stove	2	0	
1 Shovel		1	3
Total Inventory Value	192	15	10

Few changes appear to have affected the traffic department at the station over the years, although on 27.1.1930 it was agreed to provide a new warehouse in the goods yard. This was estimated by the GWR to be likely to cost £930 however, when the contract for the work was given to the firm of F. Partridge & Co. Ltd on 26.3.1931 it was valued at less than half that amount at £440. In addition a new roadway to the warehouse, additional gates and a refixed fence were necessary, costing, £157, £36 and £2, respectively.

A grimy 38xx, No. 3856 coming off the Badminton line on an up freight. In the background is the West signalbox, this time of brick construction whilst the yard is well occupied by vehicles. The water tower in the background was first referred to in correspondence around 1903, but there is conflicting evidence as to its provision at that time. It is believed to have supplied water for both station and locomotive purposes although the latter was served by just the one column located between the up line and goods yard and visible behind the train. The tank was of 22,500gall capacity at a water depth of 7ft. 6in.

R.C. Riley

An up stopping train from the South Wales line approaching Wootton Bassett in September 1955 with No. 7923 *Speke Hall* in charge. On the right the corrugated building is on part of the site of the former cattle pens and was a later addition provided for the storage of grain and animal feedstuffs. A feature on the station in the BR staff magazine for around this period revealed some interesting statistics including the fact that some 200 trains passed through the station every 24 hours. Locally in excess of 500 passengers used the station weekly and during the same period an average of 300 parcels were dealt with along with 100 tons of freight. Milk was the main traffic with nearly 15,500 galls despatched to London from the adjacent factory every week.

R.C. Riley

By 1930 the GWR had established Wootton Bassett as the centre for one of its country lorry services having a vehicle based at the station which operated over a wide area. The intention was to provide an integrated road and rail service although the limitations of both vehicle development and the general state of the roads in rural areas combined to prevent full utilisation of the service. Even so it was generally successful and the railway/lorry service can be said to have been the forerunner of today's road haulage industry.

Other than this there were a number of alterations affecting the permanent way and signalling which included additional signals and track circuits as well as a realignment of the main line junction for the South Wales line in 1937. This then allowed for 50 m.p.h. running on the Badminton route and involved the fitting of moveable elbows to the compound crossings.

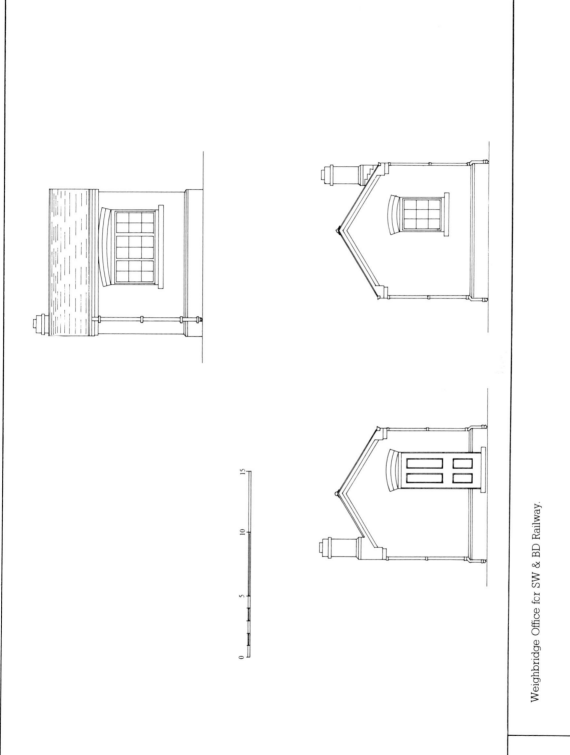

0 5 10 15

Weighbridge Office fcr SW & BD Railway.

6

WOOTTON BASSETT MILK SIDING

An interesting development at the station in 1927 was the establishment of a private siding on the Swindon side of the station and just east of the Wootton Bassett–Marlborough road overbridge. This led to a newly established milk factory operated by United Dairies and came at a time when a number of similar facilities were beginning to appear at various parts of the system in an attempt by the milk producers to increase efficiency in both milk processing and distribution compared with the previously accepted method of using churns. Milk from a large number of farms in what was then a prime dairy farming area was brought to the new factory.

As a direct comparison an entry in the records for 1910 provides an insight into the amount of churn traffic dealt with both at Wootton Bassett and the stations on the new line in the previous year.

			£	s.	d.
Wootton Bassett	93,537	churns value	5,984	3	1
Brinkworth	26,748		1,633	16	8
Little Somerford	13,722		848	3	4*
Hullavington	9,141		581	2	3
Badminton	15,440		911	2	10
Chipping sodbury	10,024		519	15	0
Coalpit Heath	1,988		59	2	1
Winterbourne	34		1	0	6

* During the same period Great Somerford on the Malmesbury Branch dealt with 6,993 churns at £420.0s.1d. (From 1933 milk previously dealt with at Great Somerford was dealt with at Little Somerford station.)

The new siding trailed away north of the up main line and took on a curved path to end parallel with the main road and thus at 90 degrees to the main line. A loop allowed for ease of working and this was modified a few years later when on 3.10.1935 approval was given for a crossover within the sidings. The cost of the modifications was estimated at £220.

The land for the new rail connection was already owned by United Dairies and this was conveyed free to the GWR in return for the provision of rail facilities; 1 acre and 32 perches being involved.

For its part, on 24.2.1927 the GWR estimated that the provision of rail facilities would cost £6,841 made up of £6,619 for civil engineering, trackwork costing £20, the

Seen from the air not long after the siding was brought into use and with the rural nature of the area being immediately apparent. The main line is out of camera running left to right whilst the siding loop and entry into the actual factory can be clearly seen.

Aerofilms

removal of existing and erection of new fencing would be £27, signalling work £150 and telegraph work £25. In the event the earthworks were contracted out to the firm of H. Smith of Newport for £4,500 and thus at a considerable saving on the original costing. The new siding was available for use from about mid-1927 despite no official siding agreement between the two parties ever appearing to have existed.

Operationally, it was for many years the practice for a locomotive to be sent light from Swindon at 1.30 p.m. daily and this then left the siding at around 2.30 p.m. with an average of thirty of the new glass-lined milk tanks – the telegraphic code of which was 'MILTA'. The train would run to West Ealing where the previously processed milk would then be bottled and sent for distribution around London. At some stage it also became the practice to shunt the 1.05 p.m. Whitland–Paddington milk train at the siding, which then collected the extra vehicles instead of running a special service. Distribution now was to a variety of the London bottling plants including South Lambeth, Queens Park, Old Ford, Bow, Clapham, Kensington and West Ealing. Other timings and destinations are also known to have existed. Empty tanks were

Photographed on the loop siding at the United Dairies depôt in 1927, is 'MILTA' No. 2004 which had a capacity of 3000 gallons contained within a glass-lined tank.

GWR Magazine

returned either direct or as a special working, i.e., the 5.40 p.m. from Westbury (ex Paddington).

Controlling the siding was a two lever Ground Frame with an Annetts Lock electrically released from the station East signalbox. Not unexpectedly precise instructions as to shunting were laid down in the Sectional Appendix and although lengthy are reproduced here in full:

The connection is in the rear of the Up Outer Advanced Starting signal for Wootton Bassett East SignalBox. The connection is controlled by a Ground Frame, known as the United Dairies Siding Ground Frame, and is electrically interlocked with Wootton Bassett East Signalbox. The siding has a connection inside the gate at the G.W. boundary with two looped siding on the United Dairies Company's property, with a capacity of about 10 tank wagons of about 25 feet length.

The United Dairies Company arrange for outwards loaded wagons to be placed for despatch on one of the sidings, and empty and other inwards wagons (1) must be placed on the inwards siding.

The Main Line at this place is on a gradient of 1 in 660, falling towards Bristol. the gradient of the Siding is 1 in 40, falling from the Factory to the Up Main Line. A spring catch point is provided between the loop and the gate at the G.W. boundary which can be held closed by a lever provided for the purpose, and must be so held by the man in charge of the shunting for movements from the looped siding towards the main line.

The Siding is under the supervision of the Station Master at Wootton Bassett.

No train must call at the Siding unless it is accompanied by a man appointed for the duty by the Wootton Bassett Station Master. When work is being done at the Siding the engine must be at the London end of the wagons.

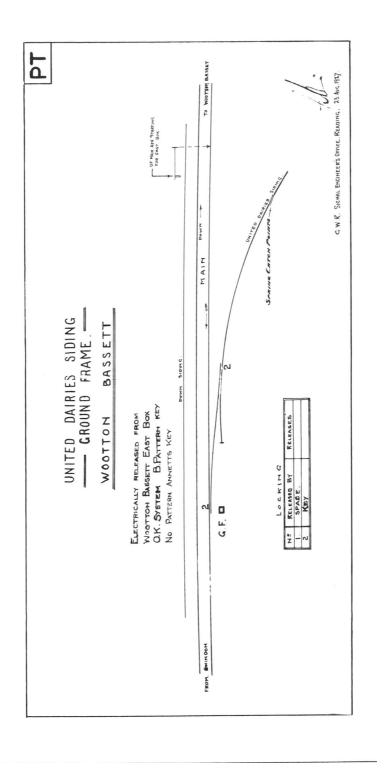

UNITED DAIRIES SIDING
— GROUND FRAME. —
WOOTTON BASSETT

ELECTRICALLY RELEASED FROM
WOOTTON BASSETT EAST BOX
O.K. SYSTEM B.PATTERN KEY
NO PATTERN ANNETTS KEY

FROM SWINDON

DOWN SIDING

UP MAIN ARM STARTING
FOR EAST BOX

TO WOOTTON BASSETT

← UP   MAIN   DOWN →

G.F. □

2

2

UNITED DAIRIES SIDING

SPRING CATCH POINTS

LOCKING

Nº	RELEASED BY	RELEASES
1	SPACE.	
2	KEY	

G.W.R. SIGNAL ENGINEER'S OFFICE, READING., 23. AUG, 1947.

PT

Telephonic Communication is provided between Wootton Bassett East Signalbox and the Ground Frame Cabin. The key of the Ground Frame Cabin must be kept in the former.

The Ground Frame is released by Lever No. 44 in Wootton Bassett East Signalbox, and when that lever is in the reverse position, the Up Starting and Advanced Starting Signals for Wootton Bassett East Signalbox are locked in the 'Danger' position.

An engine or train, of not more than 10 vehicles without a brake van, may run from Wootton Bassett East 'Box to the siding and return over the Up line under the following regulations.

The man appointed for the duty by the Wootton Bassett Station Master must come to an understanding with the Signalman at Wootton Bassett East 'Box as to the work required to be done at the Siding and must accompany the train to the Siding, riding on the last vehicle or the nearest vehicle thereto that is suitable. There must be a tail lamp on the last vehicle.

When a train is being propelled from the Siding to Wootton Bassett Station, the man appointed for the duty must ride in the leading vehicle, or if he is not able to do so, the train must be propelled at a walking pace, and he must precede the leading vehicle. He must keep a sharp look-out and be prepared to hand signal to the Driver. The speed when the train is being propelled must not exceed 10 miles per hour, and after sunset or during fog and falling snow a red lamp must be carried on the front of the leading vehicle. Before the engine or train leaves the Ground Frame for the Station, Crossover Road No. 38 must be set for the Down Main Line, or Points No. 41 must be set for the Up Siding and the appropriate signal lowered for the movement.

An Up train must not be accepted by the Signalman at Wootton Bassett East 'Box after he has given permission for an engine or engine and vehicles to return from the Siding to Wootton Bassett Station, until such engine or engine and vehicles have arrived at the Station or passed clear of the Up Main Line.

When work is completed at the Siding the man appointed for the duty must see that nothing is left foul, set the points for the Main Line, replace Lever No. 1 (to release the lock on Lever No. 44 in Wootton Bassett East Signalbox), and lock up the Ground Frame Cabin.

A through train calling at the siding to do work must be signalled in the usual way and when it has proceeded on its journey, the man appointed for the duty must inform the Signalman at Wootton Bassett East 'Box by telephone, and the latter must inform the Signalman at the box in advance.

It may well have been that a capstan or other arrangement was available for moving loaded wagons within the depôt. Details of any other traffic aside from milk to the siding are not recorded.

Interestingly the 1954 service timetables record that the following classes of engine were prohibited from the siding, BR Standard classes 6 and 7, 4 and 5 (4-6-0) and the following WR engines, 78xx, 29xx, 40xx, 39xx, 49xx, 59xx, 69xx, 47xx, 4073, 50xx, 70xx, 68xx and 10xx classes. It would appear likely then that either a small engine was used for the trips originating from Wootton Bassett necessity with an engine change at Swindon or a number of vehicles were used as a 'barrier'.

BRINKWORTH

The first station proper on the new line was at Brinkworth at 87m. 1ch. to the west of Paddington. The village of the same name lay slightly to the north of the railway and is perhaps best known for its fifteenth-century church which contains the remains of several old wall paintings. Brinkworth was also once the family home of William Penn who was renowned for his Puritan principles.

Facilities consisted of up and down platforms, each 401ft. long with the main station buildings on the up side. In design the new station buildings were of the type used almost exclusively by the GWR for small stopping places from about 1902–1917; pressed red bricks with groins and plinths in Staffordshire blues whilst window sills, heads and chimney caps were in Forest of Dean 'bluestone'.

The main buildings measured 43ft. 9in. x 10ft. and consisted of a porter's room, station master's office, general waiting room, ladies waiting room and toilet. On the

Looking west from the road overbridge towards Brinkworth station c. 1919. Visible on the right is the approach road and weighbridge hut whilst on the original print it is just possible to make out the roof of the signalmen's cottages above the roof of the hut. The lack of traffic is all too apparent although there are a number of milk churns on both platforms. The tall home signal was necessary to enable sighting over the arch of the road bridge.

L.G.R.P.

opposite platform was a small waiting shelter and toilet 22ft. 6in. x 10ft. Both structures were supported by a canopy which extended to the front and the west end. The estimated cost of each building when new was £491. 17s. 7d. and £172. 10s. 0d., respectively.

Connecting the two platforms was a metal and timber footbridge at the west end of the buildings which were erected by Pearson's from standard parts supplied by the Great Western. Board crossings for the use of the staff also existed at either end of the platforms. In keeping with most of the other stations the platform surface was paved only for part of its area the remainder consisting of a layer of stone chippings.

At the east end of the station a brick overbridge carried the Dauntsey to Swindon road over the railway, from which access was also afforded to the station. For vehicles a tree-lined approach led down from the public highway opposite the village infant school to the up side station buildings. Two metal gateposts at the top of the path bore the inscription 'T. James. Vulcan Foundry, Cardiff. 1902'. A metalled footpath provided access from the main road to the rear of the down side buildings and a number of concrete posts each with a windlass to which a pressure lantern was attached, illuminated both paths.

Continuing on from the up side approach, the roadway led on towards the small goods yard, this consisting of a single looped siding with headshunts at either end and with a small goods lock-up mid-way along. Two trailing crossovers afforded access

A contemporary postcard view of the interior of the station looking west towards Little Somerford. Of the men visible two are probably from the the permanent way gang and with what is probably one of the signalmen nearest the camera. Notice in particular the number of churns lined up against the platform fencing.

Lens of Sutton

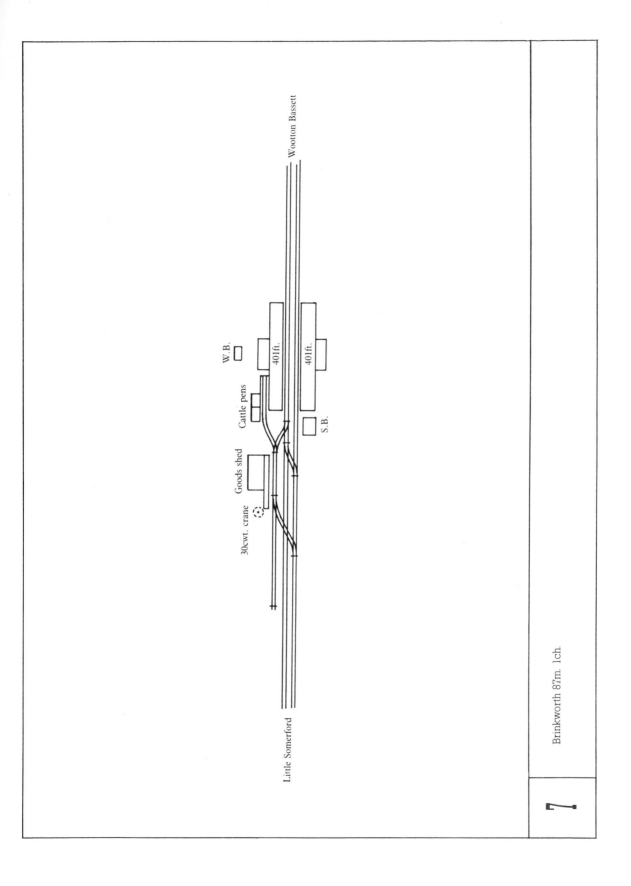

Little Somerford

Wootton Bassett

30cwt. crane

Goods shed

Cattle pens

W.B.

401ft.

401ft.

S.B.

Brinkworth 87m. 1ch.

from the running lines to the yard. The goods lock-up was identical to those at Little Somerford, Hullavington and Badminton. A set of cattle pens and carriage landing faced the headshunt nearest to the station. A 12-ton weighbridge and brick-built weigh hut stood at the entrance to the yard while at some stage a 30cwt. crane was added outside the goods lock-up alongside the siding. A total of 29 four wheeled vehicles could be accommodated on the three sidings.

Controlling the layout was a brick-built signalbox 21ft. x 12ft. x 8ft. – measured to the floor and which contained a frame of just 21 levers equipped with double twist locking at 5in. centres. Originally the 'box was manned continuously, but as early as 20.3.1910 arrangements were made for switching out at certain times as per the notice on p. 74.

Some of the intricate fretwork carvings of Signalman Plumley from Brinkworth.

GWR Magazine

In charge of the station was a station master, the first incumbent being Mr A. Barrington, who supervised two class 1 porters and three signalmen. Around 1907 one of the signalmen was Mr Plumley who came to note in the GW Staff magazine for his hobby of intricate fretwork carvings. The signalmen were classified as grade 4 by 1934. A small terrace of three cottages to the north of the goods shed facing the railway was provided by the GWR as accommodation for the signalmen. A detached house was provided for the station master at the top of the up side access alongside the main road, and was similar to the other houses provided elsewhere on the line for the station master grade. Unusally here the east wall of the house had two long lengths of bridge rail running vertically as supports, although it is not known if these were part of the original construction.

At some time prior to 1934 economy dictated that the position of station master be abolished and instead supervision was exercised from neighbouring Little Somerford. By this time also only four men worked at the station, two signalmen – brought about by the reduction in 'box hours – and the two porters. The latter acted as 'general factotums' dealing with everything from issuing tickets to loading and unloading in the yard.

For the whole of the station's life both passenger and freight traffic was light, the latter served by one up and one down pick up goods daily often on a 'CR' (call when required) basis. An amount of coal was received for the local merchant although this traffic had all but ceased by 1946. Quantities of milk in churns were forwarded by passenger service. (See Appendix B.)

Throughout the life of the station an average of four passenger trains each weekday in either direction provided the basic service with only two trains each way on Sundays.

The up pick-up goods at Brinkworth around 1937. *Dean Goods* No. 2526 in charge of a short train standing on the goods shed siding. The actual building is hidden from view behind the engine.

L. Reason

PRIVATE AND NOT FOR PUBLICATION.   Signal Notice No. S. 658.

GREAT WESTERN RAILWAY.

(For the use of the Company's Servants only.)

Additional Arrangements

FOR

Closing Signal Boxes.

The following additional arrangements for closing Signal Boxes will come into force on Sunday, March 20th.

Signal Box.	From.	To.
Bathampton ...	10.0 p.m. Sundays ...	5.0 **a**.m. Mondays.

Switch will be provided for Main Line working, and Branch will be closed.

Studley	3.0 a.m. Sundays ...	7.30 a.m. Mondays.
	3.0 a.m week-days ...	7.0 a.m. week-days.
Brinkworth ...	3.0 a.m. Sundays ...	7.0 a.m. Sundays.
	8.0 a.m. Sundays ...	7.45 a.m. Mondays.
	3.0 a.m. week-days ...	7.0 a.m. week-days.

On Mondays, Patney will be opened at 6.0 a.m. instead of 6.30 a.m., and Edington at 6.5 a.m. instead of 6.0 a.m.

Acknowledge Receipt to Head of Department.

C. KISLINGBURY,

Superintendent of the Bristol Division.

Bristol, *March 17th*, 1910.

(2,500 D. 8vo.)   Arrowsmith, Printer, Quay Street, Bristol.

LITTLE SOMERFORD

Almost seven miles from Wootton Bassett junction was the station of Little Somerford, the first of the four track stopping places on the new line. As previously recounted the prefix 'Little' was given right from the time of opening and intended to avoid confusion with the nearby station on the Malmesbury branch approximately half a mile distant. Yet, when that stopping place was closed in 1933 the prefix 'Little' was retained, remaining as such until the station's closure in 1961.

The station served the village from which its name was derived and which was just north of the line. In reality this was little more than a scattered collection of dwellings the most important being the Manor House and Rectory, both close by the railway. Great Somerford village, which was a larger community was south of the line.

This was probably taken about the time of the opening of the station and is looking towards Wootton Bassett. It has the timber and gravel surface that was typical of most of the stopping places on the new line. Deterioration in later years meant that the surface was replaced with conventional paving slabs. Identical to the buildings at Brinkworth the differing shades of brickwork show up well in the photograph, the roof is covered in 'Bangor slate'. Notice the 'spear' fencing at the rear of the platforms, that on the up side broken by a gate to allow for churns to be off-loaded directly onto the platform – a number of churns can be seen nearby. Some lime-washed cattle wagons are also just visible in the bay at the far side of the up buildings.

Science Museum/Pearson Collection

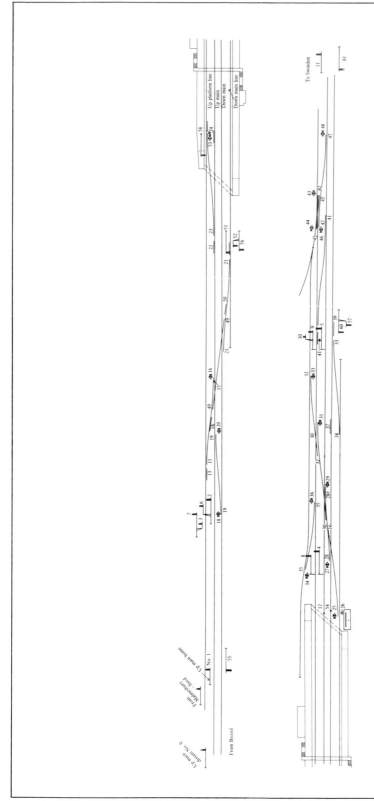

Little Somerford 1932. New diagram and changes. One lever to be added to the frame – locking to be altered. Note: A No. 59 is shown on the original adjacent to No. 51 – the reference is believed to be a drawing office error at Reading.

8

Notes on signalling diagram for Little Somerford.

Subsidiary Lights

Red – 17, 20, 25, 27
White – 34, 36, 43, 44, 46, 48

Electric Repeaters

Type	Flag	Lever No.
Arm	1	1, 55, 0
Arm	2	(2, 6) (52, 56, 59)
Light	11	(1, 2, 6, 55, 56, 59, 52, 0)
Arm & Light	1	61
	10	61

Detection – as amended

No.	Normal	Reverse
2	23	22
3	23, 49	13, 15, 14, 22
6		22, 23
7	15	13
9		40, 41
10	41	40
16		15
17		23
18		19
20		19
25	30, 32	26, 30, 32
27	30, 32	30, 32, 28
29	26	26, 28
31	26	26, 30
33	26	26, 32
34		35
36		35
43		42
44		45
46		47
48	45	45, 47
52		21, 49, 50, 51
52	23	53
58	49	21, 50, 51
57		38, 39
60	38	39

Railway facilities consisted of up and down main lines with a loop on either side fronting a platform. At the east end of the station and on the up side was a small yard, complete with goods loop, mileage siding, lock-up shed, cattle pens, loading dock and yard crane. The yard could be reached via a trailing connection from either the up or down platform loop – although the latter involved using the ladder crossing over all four running lines and so effectively 'shut up the station' completely.

Despite the fact that the station was on one of the fastest stretches of the main line, as far as most of the staff were concerned the non-stop trains were of little consequence and their lot was very much that of a country station. The exception to this was of course the signalman who had to oversee operations from a timber signalbox at the east end of the down platform.

The site of the signalbox is of particular interest for it can be seen to be almost exactly mid-way between the turnouts at the extreme ends of the station layout. This was at a time when the Board of Trade were only just beginning to accept recent advances in mechanical signalling technology and which allowed for accuracy in movement over a greater distance. Consequently the points were now a maximum distance of 880ft. from the 'box. A similar arrangement applied at several of the other stations on the new line.

Looking east but this time from further back. The line immediately in the foreground is the spur provided in 1912 as a consequence of the regular running of 60–100 wagon coal trains which would then set back slightly into the new headshunt so allowing faster trains to pass. The platform ramps can also be seen to have corrugations, a standard addition intended to assist the staff in slippery conditions.

L.G.R.P.

Many years later in 1941, the loops were extended considerably with control still exercised from the original signalbox although by now electricity was used for remote control of the points using a Westinghouse hand generator.

The signalbox, which measured 38ft. x 13ft. x 12ft. 6in. to the operating floor, originally contained a double twist frame of 61 levers at 5in. centres. It was modified in 1941 to a 78 lever frame at 4in. centres and with the then standard vertical tappet 5-bar locking.

The main passenger buildings were on the up or London bound platform and with their basic facilities of porters room, station master's office, general waiting room/booking hall, ladies room, and gents, perhaps reflecting from the outset that only a small amount of custom was expected. A small brick waiting room and toilet was the only passenger building on the down side. Linking the two platforms was a covered footbridge, the steps of which were staggered to suit the offset position of the buildings which was itself due to difficulties experienced in finding suitable footings. Indeed plans reveal that both buildings were supported on deep foundations and with the subsoil the reason why a timber and not a brick signalbox had been provided. From the original contract for the railway the cost of the station buildings and goods lock-up is quoted as identical to that at neighbouring Brinkworth.

In charge of the station was a class 4 station master who supervised two porters and

An up goods behind 28xx, No. 2880 on the main line at Little Somerford in June 1932. In the background the station nameboard was altered shortly afterwards to read '... change for Malmesbury' as the connection onto the existing branch was made the following year.

Photomatic

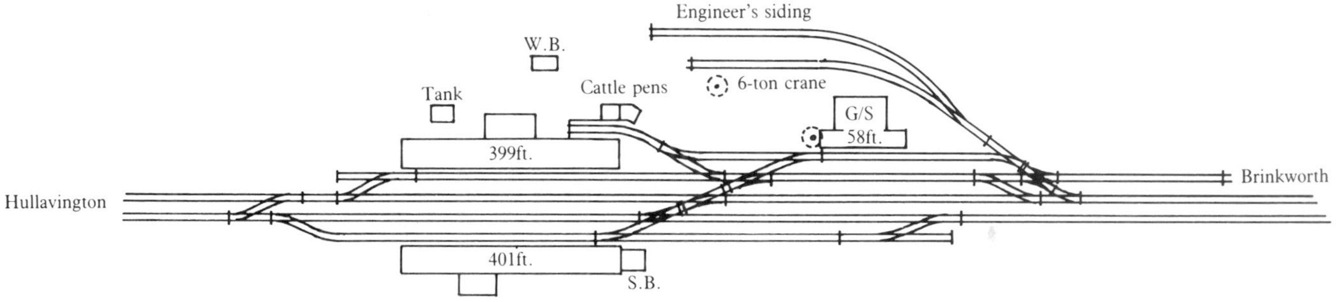
Engineer's siding
W.B.
6-ton crane
Tank
Cattle pens
G/S
58ft.
399ft.
Brinkworth
Hullavington
401ft.
S.B.

9

Little Somerford 89m. 60ch.

A Malmesbury branch service at little Somerford in August 1950. The engine is No. 5804 which would shortly run round its 'B'-set prior to returning to the branch terminus.

L.G.R.P.

three signalmen. For some years there was also a lad porter but the post was abolished about 1946 and reputedly much to the annoyance of the then station master. In addition control was exercised over two men on the Malmesbury branch, one at Great Somerford and the other at Kingsmead Mill Crossing. Accommodation for the station master was originally provided in a company house almost a third of a mile away from the station, although later a standard detached house was built nearer the station. This and a pair of semi-detached railway cottages were located in a private lane running parallel with the line just west of the station.

It appears that some difficulties were encountered in securing a suitable water supply for both the station and railway cottages, and for some time after the station opened supplies were brought in by a rail-borne tank, the churns then being taken to the railway cottages. Later an attempt was made to sink a well but analysis of the water drawn from it showed traces of several undesirable elements and the heading was rapidly filled in. Shortly afterwards in 1906, a pump house was provided adjacent to the River Avon its pipes then ran under the line west of station. This was equipped with a 'Petter' oil engine which was surplus to requirements at Southcote Junction, Reading and so allowed adequate water supplies to be provided. At the same time a water tower and columns were erected alongside the main lines. The total cost of this

Gradient profiles of the South Wales & Bristol Direct Railway (including embankments and cutting – distorted scale).

10

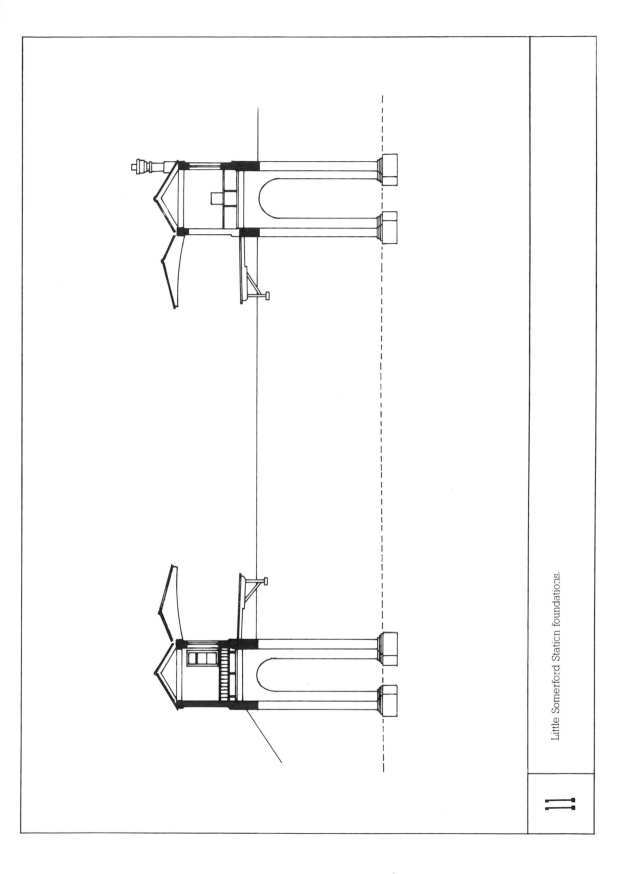

Little Somerford Station foundations.

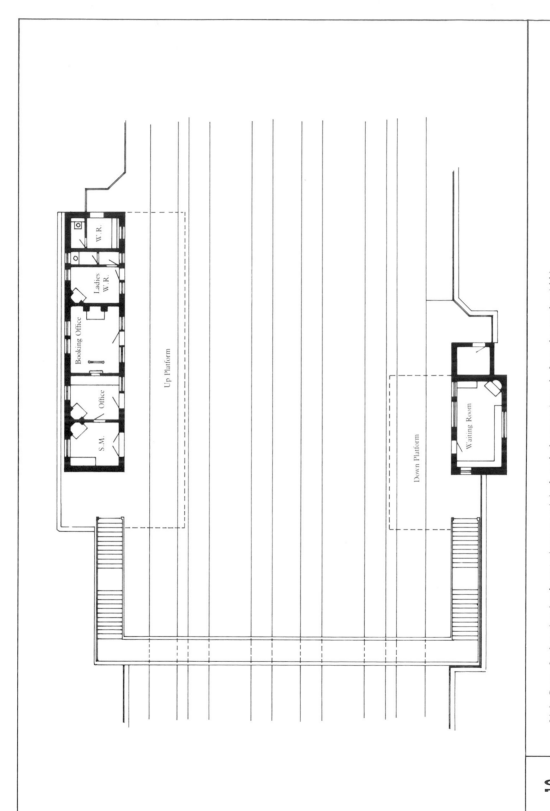

Little Somerford station (scale not given on original, scaled approximately from the track width).

12

Seen from a train on the down through line the up side buildings present a forlorn appearance in April 1961 a few days after official closure to passenger services. In the background the branch can be seen running parallel with the main line, the branch starting signal is just visible at the end of the platform.

A.E. Bennett

work was recorded as £1,695. In February 1942 an electric pump replaced the previous installation, this time at a cost of £320.

A tantalising entry in official records for March 1910 comments that signalman J. Raymond had been '. . . commended for alertness displayed in an emergency'. Regretfully though the incident itself is not recorded.

Public and vehicle access to the station was on the down side only via a long drive climbing up from the Chippenham–Swindon road which passed underneath the railway just west of the station. The approach road also led on into the goods yard, past the weighbridge, and to the goods lock-up which was identical in design to that found at Brinkworth. A 6-ton crane alongside the mileage siding and 1-ton crane next to the goods lock-up completed the facilities.

The platform loops were also used as a refuge for freight trains so leaving the main lines free. In practice it was soon found that the rear of such trains would foul the running lines and so in 1912 a short dead end siding was added at the trailing end of both up and down loops. The cost of these alterations was estimated at £364 to the engineering department and £95 for signalling.

The successor to steam on the Malmesbury goods, a service which continued to run for some years after passenger services had been withdrawn. D2187 is on the branch goods at Little Somerford prior to its journey to the terminus.

Colin Maggs

At some stage prior to 1920 an engineers siding was added north of the mileage siding which could hold a maximum of twenty-four four-wheeled vehicles. The cost of this is not recorded.

Traffic may be best described as light throughout the life of the station although an amount of livestock and milk was handled. Indeed in most years goods receipts exceeded those of passengers – see Appendix B.

An average of six passenger services in each direction served the station on weekdays together with a pick-up goods in each direction. Sundays saw just two passenger trains each way together with a single up goods working which called as required to collect any wagons of livestock ready for despatch. For most of its life the station was open from 7.00 a.m. to 7.30 p.m. daily (except Sundays) and with the two porters working alternate early and late shifts there was a period of overlap during the day.

Without doubt the major change to affect the railway throughout the life of the station was authorised in 1932. This involved the diversion of the existing Malmesbury branch via a new connection to run parallel with the South Wales main line and link in with the up platform line. With the completion of the new link the former section of the branch south towards Dauntsey was closed to passengers along with the stopping

A Britannia Pacific No. 70018 *Flying Dutchman* disturbing the peace as it approaches the station with the up 'Capitals United Express'. The train is just passing over the roadbridge west of the station which was extended in 1932 at a cost of £1,200.

T.E. Williams/National Railway Museum

place at Great Somerford. The branch was retained however for some distance as a stub siding.

An entry in official records for the new work reads as follows:

Construction of new line connecting the Malmesbury branch at Kingsmead Crossing with the South Wales main line at Little Somerford Station.

Earthwork	£2,080
Additional fencing	105
Additional drainage	200
Extension of underbridge at Little Somerford	1,200
Additional cattle grids	120
Alterations to permanent way	860
New permanent way	1,525
Land required (4a. 1r. 15p.)	380

The work was completed early the following year but owing to a legal complication was not used until Monday 17.7.1933. From this time the branch service of an engine and one or two coaches would shuttle to and from the main line and the terminus at Malmesbury, although the service lasted just 18 years for it was withdrawn by British Railways as from 10.9.1951, an early casualty of the nationalised railway network.

HULLAVINGTON

The next station west from Little Somerford was at Hullavington which besides serving the village of the same name covered an area bounded by the neighbouring villages of Corston, Stanton St Quintin, Norton and Rodbourne. However, the area could only boast a small population and even when combined yielded little in the way of traffic to the railway. Indeed the whole area traversed by the railway was sparsely populated, a fact which could not have gone unnoticed by the GWR before the line was built although it must be remembered that the railway was built primarily for the benefit of through traffic – any local trade would be a bonus.

At either end of the station area the railway crossed over a public road, that at the east end was the former public highway from Hullavington to Malmesbury, whilst at the west end it was the Hullavington to Norton road, the village from which the station took its name was just south of the railway. The bridge at the east end carried four tracks over it. Between the two bridges the railway was built up on an area of

The approach to Hullavington station from the main road. Just out of camera to the left is the station master's house and the bridge (No. 255) is of the three-arch segmental type. It was constructed in dark brick and had a maximum span of 33ft. 3in., skew span of 35ft. 2in. and headway at 20ft. 10in.

David Abbott

embankment, which extended for some considerable distance either side of the line, a permanent reminder of when the contractor had used the area as a spoil dump. In many ways the station layout and facilities were similar to those at Brinkworth although a number of additions exisited on the goods side.

Access to the station was from a tree-lined roadway sloping up from the Norton road on the north side of the line. This then opened out to the rear of the up side buildings before continuing on past the weighbridge (12-ton capacity) and a pair of coal offices which served the cattle pens and goods lock-up.

Although only up and down running lines were provided refuge sidings existed for the use of goods trains off the up line at the west end of the station and off the down line at the east end, access to both of which was via a trailing connection. The small goods yard consisted of a single goods loop with head shunt at either end and a mileage siding on the north side of the line. A total of 56 wagons could be contained within the yard whilst the refuge sidings could each accommodate a 70 wagon train. Two loading gauges protected the exit from the mileage siding and goods loop.

The standard brick waiting shelter and toilet associated with the new stations were situated on the down platform, the cost of the station buildings identical with that at Brinkworth. Linking the platforms was a covered footbridge of standard GWR design. The station layout was controlled from a timber signalbox at the London end of the

A superb view of Hullavington station taken from a contemporary postcard probably not long after the opening. The scene is looking east and the station master and three of his staff can be seen posed on the down platform. Notice the timber platform supported on what may well be old sleepers and its corresponding timber surface. This may well have been provided at a cost basis.

Lens of Sutton

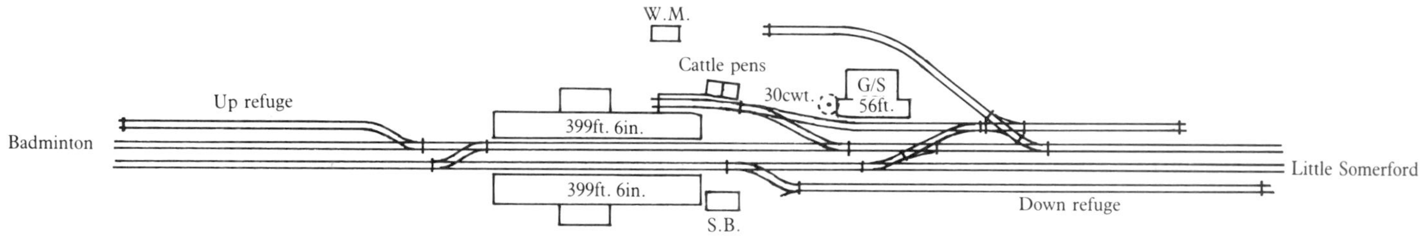

Badminton

Up refuge

W. M.

Cattle pens

30cwt.

G/S 56ft.

399ft. 6in.

399ft. 6in.

S.B.

Down refuge

Little Somerford

Hullavington (pre 1943) 94m. 20ch.

13

down platform. This was identical in design to the 'box at neighbouring Little Somerford station, although slightly smaller in size at 29ft.x 12ft. x 8ft. to the operating floor. A double twist frame with 39 levers at 5in. centres was contained within. The signalbox was provided with a block switch so that it could be switched out of circuit when traffic was light. Possibly the first time this occurred was from 3.7.1910 when the 'box was closed from 3.0 a.m. to 7.0 a.m. weekdays and 3.0 a.m. to 7.30 a.m. Sundays. Later this was varied so that the 'box was open continuously.

The traffic dealt with was similar to that at Little Somerford, although larger quantities of coal were handled with the local merchant, Messrs Wilson & Son, operating over a wider area. Parcels traffic too was at a higher level. Unfortunately, in keeping with the general national trend receipts diminished considerably from about 1938 onwards. (See Appendix B.)

The station was initially staffed by a station master, two porters and two signalmen. A substantially-built company house alongside the station approach road was provided for the station master, with a pair of cottages for the two signalmen nearby. By 1934 one of the porters had been dispensed with and his place taken by a third signalman, the GWR board approving the construction of an additional house for the new post on 15.12.1938 at a cost of £550. It would appear that all the railway houses initially provided along the line were probably built by a local contractor rather than Pearson's

Seen from the other side in the last years of the station's life the timber platform by now replaced by masonry. The soot staining from countless passing trains on the footbridge is obvious whilst the timber hut next to the footbridge was a 'BR' addition.

Colin Maggs

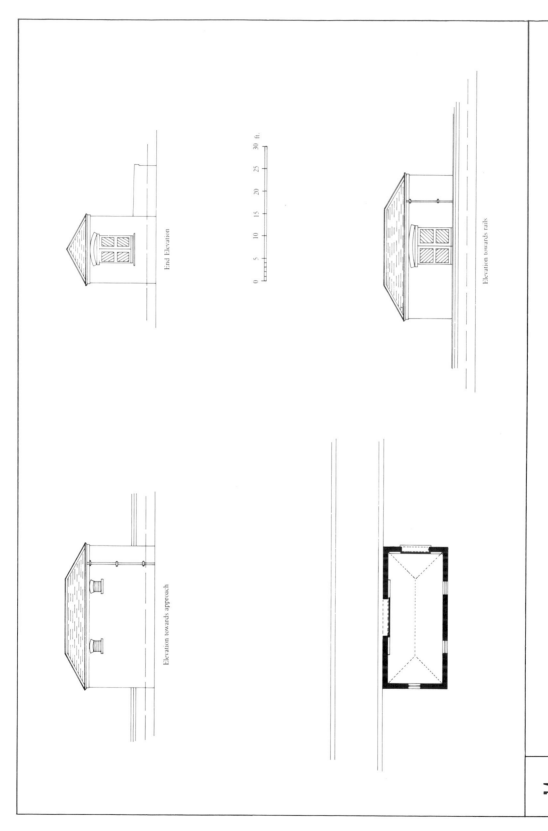

End Elevation

Elevation towards rails

Elevation towards approach

0 5 10 15 20 25 30 ft.

Goods lock-ups at Brinkworth, Somerford, Hullavington and Badminton.

14

The weighbridge hut and petrol store at Hullavington, the former constucted with a brick floor. The petrol store was provided in consequence of the country lorry being based at the station.

David Abbott

as the design does not appear elsewhere on the GWR system. Likewise it would appear that only the station master and signalmen's grades warranted a railway house.

During the 1930s a country lorry service was based at the station with a consequent increase in staff of a motor driver. (It is likely that this was one of the Badminton vehicles re-allocated.) During World War II the driver was assisted by an adult 'vanguard', whilst in keeping with most of the other stations on the line at this time female labour, usually clerks and porters, also worked on the railway.

Alterations to the signalling and layout took place in 1938 when track circuiting was provided together with an additional up outer home signal and detonator placing levers. The cost of these changes was estimated at £280. Three years later in 1941 both the refuge sidings were provided with a facing connection to allow for more flexibility in working, the necessary additions made to the signalling at the same time. A further change was the extension of the down loop around the rear of the platform and signalbox and now covered a total distance of just over half a mile. All this work may well have been instigated at the request of the Government as no detailed entry to cover the work appears in the 'Engineering Department Schedule of New Works' for the period. Both the new connections were operated by a hand generator. Shortly

No. 5060 *Earl of Berkeley* passing Hullavington in excess of 80 m.p.h. with the London bound
'Bristolian' express. The line nearest the camera is the down goods loop which continues on past the
signalbox – just visible in the background, around the rear of the down platform.

M.W. Earley

afterwards two additional sidings were provided in the yard north of the mileage
siding. Both of these are still in existence today even if in somewhat neglected
condition. Local passenger and goods services at Hullavington were similar to those
which served adjacent stations.

BADMINTON

The best known of the stations on the line must be that at Badminton. Indeed the railway was often known as the 'Badminton Line' – the station name is derived from the villages of Great and Little Badminton as well as the famous country house nearby, the ancestral seat of the Duke and Duchess of Beaufort.

In design the track layout was similar in many respects to that at Little Somerford, with through up and down lines, platform loops and a small yard at the east end of the station on the north side of the main line. The arrival of the railway produced an unexpected spin-off for the village as they now found themselves connected to a

A superb official study of the station, looking westward and taken around the time of opening. Under a glass it is possible to discern that one of the posters on the up side building is in fact announcing the opening of the new Badminton station and South Wales direct line. The photograph provides a wonderful degree of detail and it also reveals a somewhat unusual GWR monogram on the station seats as well as the station lamps each with their opaque plaque engraved with the station name. Notice too the platform surfaces which are of masonry, no doubt a reflection of the importance of the station. At the time the photograph was taken the station master's house had yet to be erected but would occupy a site to the left of the down side approach path.

British Railways

Carved in limestone and mounted on the end wall of the station building, the crest of the Duke of Beaufort. Besides the royal train journey referred to on p. 15, Queen Mary was a regular user of the station. She would be met by car on arrival from London and her equerry would telephone the station from Badminton House to announce Her Majesty was en route to the railway

Adrian Vaughan

running water supply for the first time in Badminton – this came courtesy of the West Gloucester Water Co. who had provided a supply to the contractors at the time of construction.

The main station buildings were on the up side with a public access from here to the down platform via a covered footbridge. Difficulties in securing the necessary depth of foundations meant that, as at Brinkworth, deep piles were driven some distance into the ground to support the up and down buildings. Both waiting rooms were equipped with the latest type of 'slow-burning' solid fuel stove and oil lighting. A change to electricity was not made until late 1937 and then at a recorded cost of £191.

Despite the similarity in general building style used throughout the line, at Badminton a number of changes were made. These included the use of more glass in the platform canopies to give a lighter and more airy appearance whilst the coat of arms of the Duke of Beaufort was also represented on a limestone plaque mounted on the west end of the up side building.

The siting of the station meant that it was ideally placed to serve the villages of Nettleton, Acton Turville, Burton and of course Badminton. The Acton Turville to Badminton road passed over the railway at the west end of the station on a well proportioned girder bridge which had a span of 40ft. 6in. with a skew span of 46ft. 9in. It was supported on brick piers 14ft. 7in. above rail level. From this road a driveway led down on either side to both the up and down buildings; that on the down

The station master's accommodation at Badminton. There were two basic designs of station house on the main line, this being the larger type which also appeared at Chipping Sodbury, such facilities no doubt reflecting the importance of the actual stopping places.

D.V. Abbott
Courtesy of Mr & Mrs Saunders

side terminating at the rear of the waiting rooms although the approach on the up side continued on towards the goods yard. Access to the down side platform was via a gate alongside the bottom of the footbridge steps. The traffic facilities were added to in 1947 when on 12 June approval was given for, '. . . an improvement to the parcels office and cycle storage accommodation', at an estimated cost of 730. The new work involved a substantial brick structure adjoining the east end of the up main platform building and included a canopy. Cycle storage had previously been in a corrugated iron hut.

Traffic at the station was second only to that at Chipping Sodbury and included a reasonable number of passengers as well as horse-box traffic, coal for the local merchant, a Mr Silvey, and general agricultural produce, particularly fertilizer and straw. It has been suggested that Silvey's may at one time have operated their own railway wagons, in a red and white livery, although this cannot be confirmed.

Indeed between 1913 and 1925 the number of tickets issued was in excess of five figures. The station was also unique in that in the first eleven months of 1946 it was the

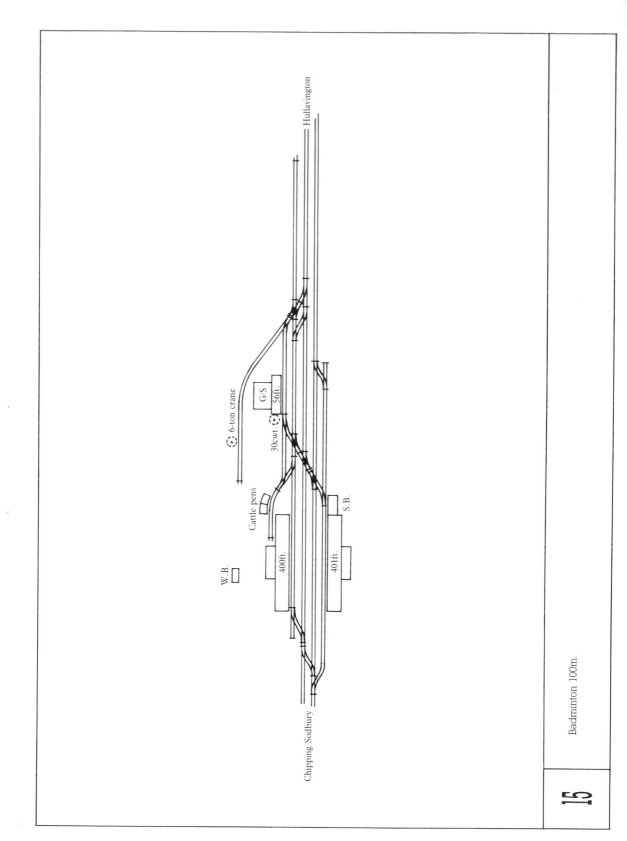

Hullavington

6-ton crane

G/S

56ft.

30cwt.

Cattle pens

S.B.

W.B.

400ft.

401ft.

Chipping Sodbury

Badminton 100m.

15

only one of the seven stopping places to show an increase in all types of traffic compared with the corresponding period in 1938.

Under a covenant signed in 1899 between the Duke of Beaufort and the GWR the railway agreed to stop four passenger trains each way daily at the station and in addition any train had to stop at Badminton if a first class passenger wished to alight. A side effect of this arrangement was that apart from the usual stopping passenger services several 'fasts' were booked to call at the station, while a notice as to the provisiors for first class passengers to alight if they so desired was included in the public timetables. From a survey of traffic on the line during its first year of operation it appears that sixty passenger services were run which terminated at Badminton and it may well have been that these were special workings in connection with the renowned Badminton Hunt. Visitors to the hunt would often stay at the privately owned Portcullis Hotel which had been built at the same time as the railway and was situated on the south side of the line a short distance from the down side entrance. The periodical *Fieldens Magazine* suggested at the time that the Hotel was built in such close proximity to the railway thereby negating the need for any special waiting rooms or other accommodation for the use of huntsman at the station. Evidently great things were hoped for with the hotel and an advert appeared in the first edition of *Holiday Haunts* (see p. 101). This would appear to have been one of the few times the location was mentioned in the guide although it remained as a hotel until the 1930s when it was converted into a number of permanent residences.

Indeed the importance of the station in relation to hunt traffic can be gauged when it is realised that for many years a 'Hound Van' was stabled at the station and used to transport the dogs to distant hunts. The hound van would be incorporated in a special train usually consisting of two passenger coaches and sufficient horse-boxes to cater for the number of equines being taken. A notice in the working timetables for the line and issued to all staff read:

> Every care should be taken to avoid running over packs of hounds,
> which, during the hunting season may cross the line. All servants
> of the railway are hereby enjoyed to use every care consistant
> with a due regard being paid to the proper working of the line
> and trains.

A direct reference to the Badminton Hunt.

Another reflection of the importance of the station was in the number of staff employed. The figures were as follows:

1 station master – class 3
1 general clerk (junior)
2 porters – class 2
1 goods porter
3 signalmen – class 4
2 motor drivers.

A recently discovered view of the station taken from the roadbridge probably between 1906 and 1912. The 'Saint' class engine on the right is on a westbound stopping passenger whilst the down goods is probably on the daily pick-up service and in the process of shunting the yard.

Lens of Sutton

Similar to the previous view but taken in 1919 after the headshunts were added at the trailing end of each loop. Besides the tidy appearance of the trackwork the nearby grass banks also provide the same neat look although now complemented by a number of young trees.

L.G.R.P.

BADMINTON

On the new main route to South Wales and the West.

TWO HOURS FROM PADDINGTON.

The HEADQUARTERS of FOX HUNTING.

. . . THE . . .

Portcullis Hotel,

CLOSE TO G. W.
RAILWAY STATION,

and

ONE MILE

from the FAMOUS BADMINTON KENNELS.

STANDING in its own grounds of about 9 acres, recently erected and furnished with a view to affording the maximum of comfort and convenience for HUNTING QUARTERS, and commanding an ideal country for a Summer Holiday. Near the BEAUTIFUL

PARK OF BADMINTON. Open to Visitors.

By permission of HIS GRACE THE DUKE OF BEAUFORT, the Stables, Kennels, the Park and Gardens, can be viewed by Visitors to the PORTCULLIS HOTEL, for whom Guides are provided.

The Hotel Stables have been constructed with special care.

FIFTY LOOSE BOXES.

GOLF in BADMINTON PARK.   CRICKET. TENNIS. CROQUET.

MODERATE TERMS.   Express Trains stop by arrangement.

Telephone : No. 5, Badminton Post Office.
Telegrams : " STOVIN, BADMINTON."
Station : G.W.R., Badminton.

R. STOVIN, Manager.

Reproduced from the 1906 edition of *Holiday Haunts on the Great Western Railway.*

Collection of R. Youngman

Despite being heavily retouched this is an irresistable view of a number of the station staff probably taken prior to 1914. The wagons on the down through line are an interesting selection although it is not possible to tell if the train is complete or if shunting is taking place.

L.G.R.P.

The Portcullis Hotel, Badminton from an original postcard.

Kevin Robertson

Looking east from the end of the platforms the empty goods yard is in view. To the extreme left is the engineers siding and it is just possible to discern the goods lock-up and crane as well as the railway cottages on the opposite side of the line. Notice too the centre-pivot signals – there were a number at the station.

British Railways

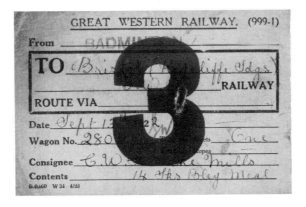

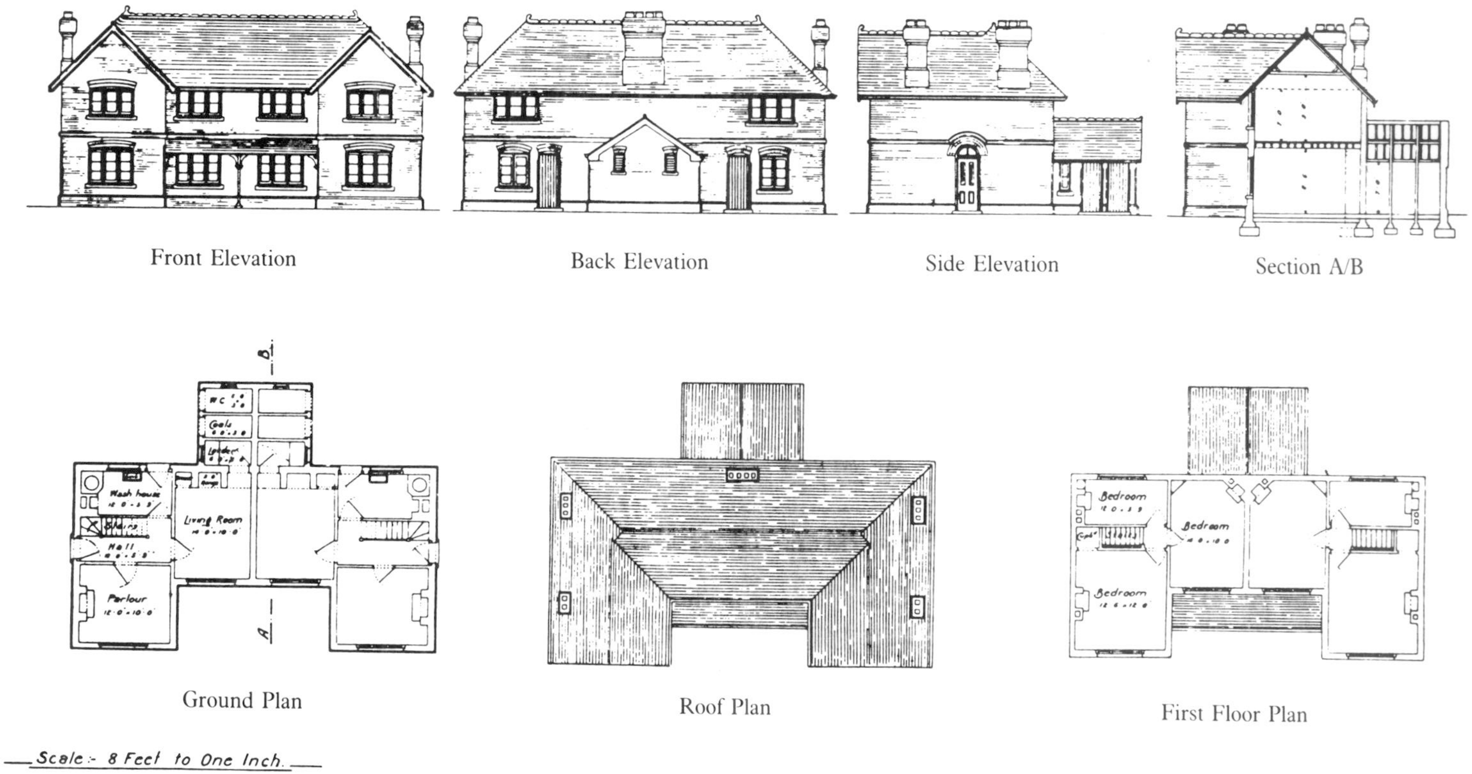

Section A/B

First Floor Plan

Side Elevation

Back Elevation

Roof Plan

Front Elevation

Ground Plan

Scale :- 8 Feet to One Inch.

CWRSW & BD Railway signalmen's cottages at Badminton.

16

The GWR Country Lorry service at Badminton in February 1928 which at the time brought in over 700 gallons of milk daily to the station from farms within a 5m. radius. The cost of the service to the producer was ½d. per imperial gallon. 'XT 6394' is a 'AEC' vehicle and is fitted with acetylene headlights and solid tyres; notice also the warning horn and radiator blind. On the side of the vehicle was affixed a standard notice which read 'GWR Country Lorry Service. This lorry will collect and deliver from and to all parts of the district. Apply to Goods Agent, Badminton'. It may well have been that the churns were destined to be loaded into the 'Siphon' in the loading dock which can be seen with its side doors open. (At least two of the large 'Siphon J' vans, Nos. 2049/50 were branded to work between Badminton and Paddington for the conveyance of churn traffic.)

British Railways

Here too the importance placed on those passengers and related traffic using Badminton station may be reflected in a 1947 memorandum on staff economies and in which the discussion point had been to replace an adult clerk with a junior: '. . . the present traffic does not justify retention of the woman clerk but having regard to the influential type of passenger using the station, it is felt that the remaining clerical post should be class 5 (instead of junior as in 1938) to ensure satisfactory service.'

A detached house for the station master was on a large plot immediately adjacent to the down side approach whilst two blocks of semi-detached railway cottages (presumably for the signalmen but different in design to those at Brinkworth, Little Somerford and Hullavington), occupied a site on the same side of the line but just east

A hound van of the type referred to in the text. The GWR possessed two such vehicles, both built in the 1880s, one with four and the other with six wheels. Each contained a separate, small compartment for the accompanying 'terrier' seen here in the lower body side just above the left hand axle. The photograph was taken at Swindon.

British Railways

'XT 6394' and a 4-ton Thorneycroft PB forward control lorry, 'YE 5406' in the down yard at the station in February 1928. The importance of milk traffic here was the reason for two vehicles being based at the station, each with their own driver who was also responsible for minor servicing. Notice the two distinct types of churn, the conical design being the older style. Unfortunately the exact date of the start of the railway lorry service has not been found although it is believed to have been around 1927/8. In BR days the lorry service was withdrawn and from that time parcels deliveries were undertaken by a Chippenham based vehicle. It is also just possible to identify the signalmen's cottages in the background.

British Railways

of the station. For some years access to these was via a footpath from the down side approach road with a path which also led to the nearby signalbox.

The signalbox itself was a brick building at the London end of the down platform and was in continuous use. A lamp hut was provided on the opposite side of the line next to the cattle pens. The station was also the home base for Bristol Division permanent way gang No. 67 whose area covered a two mile section from 98m. 30ch to 100m. 70ch.

Goods facilities included some cattle pens which faced onto a dead end siding running parallel with the London end of the up platform. An end loading dock and carriage shoot was included in this siding and with the proximity of Badminton House it is likely to have seen an amount of traffic. Adjacent to the cattle pens was a small coal store and the aforementioned lamp hut, a number of merchants offices and a private weighing machine were positioned at the edge of railway property behind the cattle pens. A little further into the yard was the standard goods lock-up and loading platform associated with the line whilst outside was a 30cwt. yard crane. A further crane, this time of 6-tons capacity was located alongside the mileage siding. It is likely the end loading dock was where the hound van was stored. A weighbridge opposite the up side building completed the facilities.

The front view of the 1947 extension to the main building which was used for parcels and cycle storage. Care was obviously taken to ensure a match with the existing canopy along the front athough the whole structure would appear to be pitched slightly higher than the original.

Courtney Haydon

Taken from the up side approach and a rear view of the extension. The gates allowed direct access onto the platform for parcels and other heavy items and would appear to be in the same position as seen originally in the official view of the station when it opened. (This photograph was taken some years after closure.)

Courtney Haydon

This is the down side passenger approach and has been included to show how the canopy was extended over the passenger access and also afforded protection to the footbridge steps. A similar arrangement existed on the Up side at Badminton and it is believed like facilities were provided at all the other stations on the new line.

Courtney Haydon

A decidedly scruffy No. 5971 *Merevale Hall* in the down goods loop at Badminton in 1963. The engine is awaiting a path onto the main line with the signal against the train although clear for the through route.

Adrian Vaughan

At some time during the 1920s a code of signals was established for communication between the signalman and shunters for movements at the west end of the yard. Why such a system was needed in view of the limited freight traffic the station handled and the clear view the signalman had of shunting operations is unclear:

Call attention – 1 beat
Set points for dead end of loop or vice versa – 2 beats
Set points up main line to loop or vice versa – 3 beats
Set points up main line to yard – 4 beats.

The original track layout included a shunting spur at the London end of the goods yard. In 1912, as with neighbouring Little Somerford, the ends of the loops were provided with a dead end siding, the cost recorded as £364 against the engineering department and £95 for signalling additions. A further addition sometime after 1920 was a short new siding at the same level as the approach road and towards the merchants offices. Its use is uncertain and it was officially removed on 20.7.1941. On the same date both the loops were extended eastwards to a maximum of 600ft. Control of the points at the far end of the extended loops was now by hand generator from the signalbox.

Badminton signalbox on a wet July day in 1968. The 'box was 38ft. x 13ft. x 10ft. 6in. in size, measured to the floor, and in its final years was given the identification 'BM' shown on the small plate above the conventional cast nameboard.

Adrian Vaughan

Inside the signalbox which displayed a high level of cleanliness right up to the time of closure. Pictured is part of the double twist locked lever frame of 61 levers at 5in. centres. Badminton and Chipping Sodbury were the only 'boxes on the line not to have a block-switch fitted which meant that they at least had to be open for the passage of all trains. On the block shelf modernisation has arrived in the form of the dialled train describer, although to the right the glass covered time release instruments remain. These were intended to be used in connection with the motor points although the 3-min timer they contained was more useful for assessing when a breakfast boiled egg was cooked!

Adrian Vaughan

Against the background of an evening sky, the last rays of the setting sun highlight a Pembroke Dock–Paddington express speeding through the station in June 1952. During the 1950s 'The Red Dragon' express was scheduled to stop at the station but only in the down direction, its only booked call between Swindon and Newport.

G.F. Heiron

CHIPPING SODBURY

Whilst neighbouring Badminton may have been the best known of all the stations it was Chipping Sodbury that was without doubt the busiest, having receipts which during most years were equal to the combined total of all the other stations on the line. (See Appendix B).

In design the station layout was similar to that at Badminton but with the addition of extra facilities for goods traffic. These are shown on the accompanying track plan.

The station served the small town of the same name which was situated approximately half a mile from the railway, which at the time of opening was home to some 1500 persons. It is interesting to note that in 1901 at the time the signalbox nameplates were ordered for the new railway, the original plate for the 'box was quoted as 'Sodbury Signal Box'. It is likely this name was taken from the manor house of

A superb view of the station taken soon after its opening and looking east. Already a number of goods vehicles are visible in the yard and the signals have been pulled off in anticipation of a train on the up platform line. Notice the paving slabs and stone of the platform which were a mixture of Hippsholme (York) and Groby (Leicestershire) patent stone. On the left, is the pathway running down the cutting side which led down onto the railway from the engineer's offices.

Science Museum/Pearson Collection

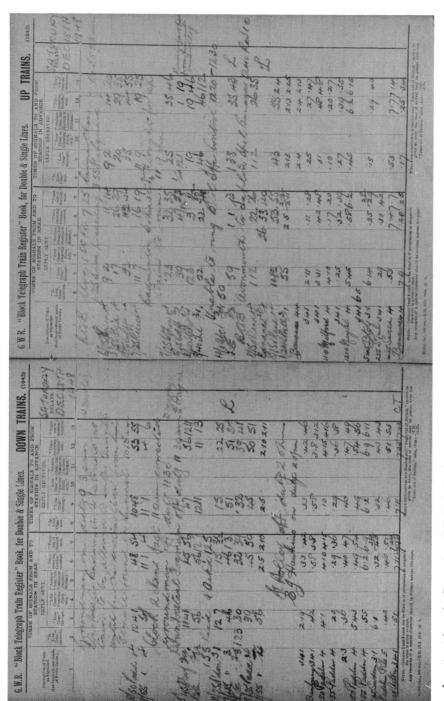

An extract from the December 1948 Train Register for Chipping Sodbury with the obvious lack of traffic a matter of interest. At the top of the down side page is an entry which reads, 'Groundsman on duty 9.30 a.m. Stn. Master Badminton instructs no train to be allowed to enter tunnel until further instructed from him. Female found in tunnel 10.15 a.m.'

Courtesy of Alan Price

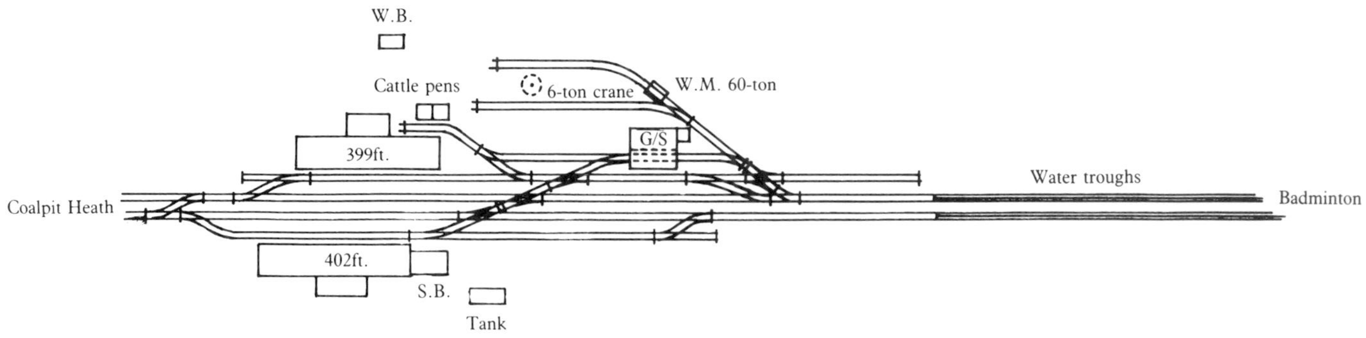

Coalpit Heath

W.B.

Cattle pens

399ft.

G/S

6-ton crane

W.M. 60-ton

Water troughs

Badminton

402ft.

S.B.

Tank

Chipping Sodbury 104m. 46ch.

17

Taken around the same time as the previous view but this time looking to the west. On the up side the buildings are left to right, the station master's office, parcels office, clerks (booking office) – entrance in waiting room – ladies and gents. Behind the main buildings the corrugated structure is the former resident engineer's office which was later demolished.

British Railways

'Sodbury Hall' one mile from the line. It was here that William Tyndale, while tutor to the children of Sir John Walsh, translated the Bible into the English language at the beginning of the sixteenth century. Since that time, however, the building has been just a farmhouse although the old chapel still remains. The site of an old Roman encampment was also situated nearby. By 1903 however the designation of 'Chipping Sodbury' had been decided upon.

Access to the station was via a long approach from the Chipping Sodbury to Old Sodbury road, which paralleled the railway on the north side of the line. This arrived at the rear of the up side buildings with sufficient turning space for cabs before continuing on at right angles into the goods yard area. Much of the station site was excavated within a cutting of varying depth and hence no direct road or pedestrian access was available to the down side platform. Also the main buildings at this station were the largest on the line, although on the down side these were restricted to the standard waiting room and toilet. Details of the rooms and facilities are given in the

GREAT WESTERN RAILWAY.

(903)

AN AGREEMENT made the *Eighth* day of *December* One thousand *nine hundred and eight*

Between the Great Western Railway Company (hereinafter called "the Company"), by *Charles Edmund Wildsmith*

their District Goods Manager, of the one part, and *Frank Herbert Bees of Chipping Sodbury in the County of Gloucestershire*

(hereinafter called "the Agent") of the other part.

1. The said *Frank Herbert Bees* hereby agrees to become Carting-Agent to the Company for the Station and District of *Chipping Sodbury* and the Company agrees to employ the said *Frank Herbert Bees* as Carting-Agent on the following conditions :—

2. The said Agent hereby undertakes to find, in sufficient quantities, all requisite and suitable Stock in Vans, Carts, Trolleys, Timber Carriages, Horses, Harness, Pulleys, Ropes, and other necessary appliances ; to employ proper, civil, energetic, and trustworthy Men, to the satisfaction of the Company, for the collection of Goods and Merchandise within the said District, and for the delivery thereof to or from the said Station, and to remove such Men, Horses, or Vehicles, as may from time to time be considered by or on behalf of the Company to be objectionable or unsuitable.

3. The said Agent, as and when required, shall and will provide a suitable and convenient Office or Receiving House, and shall have painted in a bold and legible manner in some public and conspicuous part thereof the words "Great Western Railway Company," " *F. H. Bees* Agent," and shall also have the same words legibly painted on the sides or fixed covers of all Vehicles used or kept under or in pursuance of this Agreement.

4. Within the Free Cartage District hereinafter specified the said Agent is not to make or collect any additional charge for Collection, Delivery, Booking, or other service, over and above the Company's charges on the Goods entrusted to him, when invoiced or to be charged at "Carted" rates, except as may be herein provided for.

5. The Free Cartage District for the *Town* of *Chipping Sodbury* shall extend from the Station *within an area bounded by Yate Station in one direction through the Main Street, and including side streets, and Old Sodbury in the other direction, also to include Messrs Pernetts Brewery in the Old Sodbury Road*

From the vantage point of the brick bridge at the west end of the station and 40ft. above rail level a panoramic view can be obtained. Besides the passenger accommodation the pump house – originally operated by an acetylene-burning engine – and water tower are visible on the right whilst the yard and mileage siding are seen prior to the additions that took place from 1921 onwards.

Lens of Sutton

photograph caption on p. 115. Platform surfaces were of paving slabs throughout and with stone chips behind.

The goods facilities included a large brick goods shed with office attached as well as cattle pens, weighbridge and 6-ton yard crane. The original 12-ton weighbridge survived until early in 1954 when it was replaced by a 20-ton machine at a cost of £1,134. Furthest north in the yard was a mileage siding able to accommodate 18 wagons. Next to this was a concrete landing area and on the exit from the siding there was a 60-ton capacity weighing machine which was capable of dealing with wagons of a maximum axle spacing of 19ft. 11in. Such a facility was provided because of the amount of stone traffic using the station which was responsible for a considerable percentage of the accrued revenue. Even so other traffic was handled as witness a letter of congratulation sent to Paddington and published in the *GWR Magazine* for May 1923:

'I am pleased to say that we had the goods (a truck of furniture from Chipping Sodbury to Guernsey, via Weymouth) on Saturday and there was not a single thing broken.'

From Mr C.E. Allen, Le Platon, Guernsey to the Station Master at Chipping Sodbury.

From the earliest days the GWR awarded a cartage agency at the station giving the holder sole rights over the delivery and collection of items within a set area. As an example some of the holders of this privilege were as below:

8.12.1908 Frank Bees
23.9.1926 William Short
2.10.1926 Henry Cox

By 1938 the service was operated by the railway itself under their 'country lorry' service. A vehicle was based at the station and one of the porters would act as 'vanguard' when required. An amount of traffic was also generated in the 1940s from a government store nearby.

Due to the amount of goods traffic handled increases were made to the siding facilities very early on, including a new loading bank and siding in 1907 which was followed by a small petrol depôt in 1913. There was also an oil tank siding believed to have been to the north of the site of the original cattle pens.

It was the stone traffic that was responsible for a considerable extension of the yard facilities from 1921 onwards and involved the firm of John Arnold & Sons of Barn Hill Quarry. (Stone was handled at the station from very early on, although it was not until about 1921 that Arnold's became involved.) Commencing on 5.5.1921 the GWR minute books record approval being given to strengthening the loading bank to enable the firm to load stone from steam tip wagons directly into rail vehicles. A noteworthy addition to this was that Messrs Arnold would advance the cost of the work, estimated at £200, which would then be refunded to them at a rebate of 2s. per truck off the traffic loaded at the station. A little later in March 1926 the loading bank was raised and extended at a cost of £675. Again this was as a consequence of the stone traffic and a similar financial deal was arranged with Messrs Arnold. The final addition for the stone traffic was approved on 28.7.1927 and consisted of three extra sidings to hold a total of 44 wagons with an extension of the loading bank. To accommodate this an amount of new earthwork was involved, necessitating other slewings which involved the demolition of the existing permanent way inspector's office. A replacement building was provided on a new site. Two of the new sidings were north of the existing mileage siding with the net result that four sidings were now available purely for the stone traffic.

A set of bell codes was arranged between the signalman and shunter for movements at the east end of the yard and which were principally concerned with the stone traffic:

Call attention	1 beat
Set points up goods to platform line	2 beats
Set points up goods to back road	4 beats

In charge of the station was a class 3 station master, who in 1934 supervised a staff of 12 men.

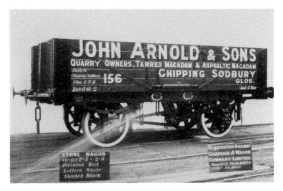

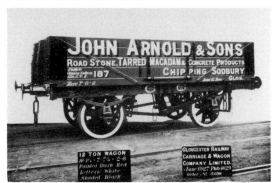

Official views of three of the vehicles owned by John Arnold & Sons.
G.R.C.W. Co.

1 General clerk, class 5
3 Porters, two class 2 and one junior
1 Goods checker
3 Signalmen (Westerleigh Junction West, class 4)
3 Signalmen, station
1 Signal lampman

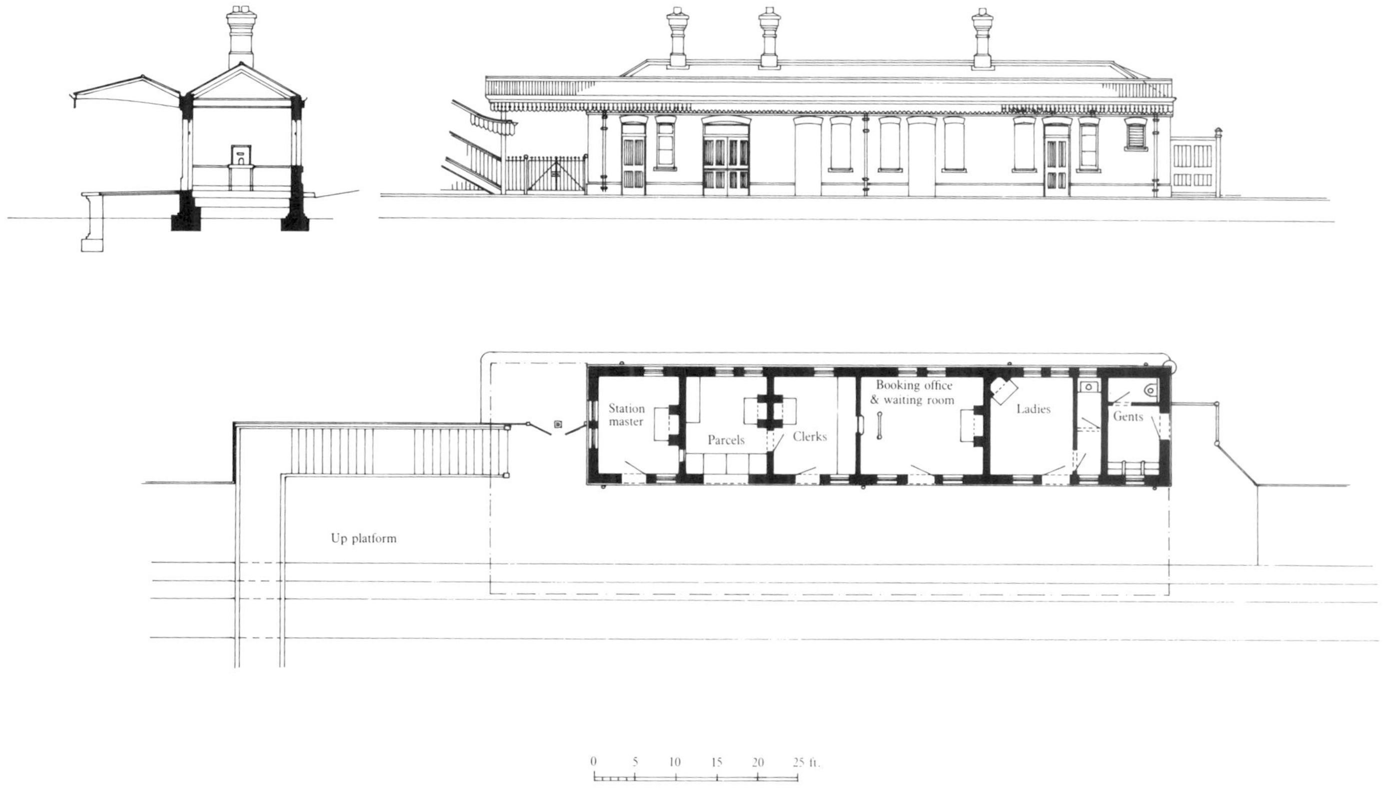

Station master

Parcels

Clerks

Booking office
& waiting room

Ladies

Gents

Up platform

0 5 10 15 20 25 ft.

Chipping Sodbury.

18

The 'fly' or pick up goods as it was known shunting at the station on 30.6.1925. The engine is No. 1005, formerly MSWJ No. 21. with at least the first four wagons of the train being private owner vehicles owned by John Arnold & Sons. In the background is the commodious goods shed where a set of re-railing ramps were stored to be used in the event of a minor miscalculation during shunting.

H. G. W. Household

The station master and four of his staff were each provided with company houses at weekly rents of 5s. 6d. and 3s. 6d. respectively. A further detached house, similar to that available to the station master, was provided for the permanent way inspector responsible for the railway. This was first occupied in 1904, again at a 5s. 6d. rental. Piped water became available to the station and houses approximately 12 months after the railway was opened.

It would appear that for some years an annual dinner was held for the traffic and permanent way staff at the station, the first one being held in 1909.

A glance at the traffic statistics in Appendix B reveals how staff wages had increased over the years; a porter being paid just 18s. a week in 1914 whilst the lampman who was responsible for the lamps over most of the line received 27s.

The signalbox at the station was a brick structure very similar to others on the railway and was 38ft. x 13ft. x 9ft. 6in. to the operating floor. It contained a double twist locking frame of 61 levers at 5in. centres, the signalman being graded class 4 under the 'marks' system. In this the number of movements daily, (referring to levers,

The replacement permanent way inspector's office which is believed to have been erected some time before 1927. Compared with the original building in mellow brick this new structure was austere yet functional although a cold water tap was provided. An interesting item concerning the engineering department at Chipping Sodbury appeared in the August 1911 *Great Western Magazine*, when it was reported that, 'Mr E. Lucas of Chipping Sodbury who recently left the service for an appointment in West Africa, has been presented by Permanent Way Inspector J. Byles, on behalf of his colleagues, with a fountain pen and smoker's outfit as momentoes of his 15 years association with them; speeches were made by Messrs Simmonds, Cox and Vickery.'

British Railways

bells, instruments, telephones, etc.) was assessed and a classification given. Fortunately a train register for the 'box for 1948 has also survived and it makes interesting reading. One surprising feature is the limited number of trains recorded as using the route at this time.

The platform loops were extended with a headshunt at either end in 1912 at a cost of £344 for engineering department work and £85 for changes and additional signalling. A further extension was built in early 1943 when the up loop was extended at both ends, and the remote control of the turnouts was exercised from the signalbox with a hand generator. No changes were made to the down side loop.

Despite the fact that Chipping Sodbury handled the most traffic there was no country lorry service based at the station. It is likely, however, Badminton based

The London bound 'Red Dragon' service passing through Chipping Sodbury in September 1952 behind No. 70028 *Royal Star*. The yard can be seen to be full of wagons and the additional sidings provided over the years are also visible. A number of other buildings can also be seen in the yard, including offices for the ganger, permanent way blacksmith and goods checker.

G.F. Heiron

vehicles would cover any tasks arising from Chipping Sodbury. Similarly no railway 'bus services operated in the area although by 1932 the rival Bristol Omnibus Company provided a number of regular turns which included:

Service 31:	Bristol – Coalpit Heath – Chipping Sodbury – Malmesbury
Service 32:	Bristol – Coalpit Heath – Chipping Sodbury – Tetbury
Service 131:	Bristol – Coalpit Heath – Chipping Sodbury

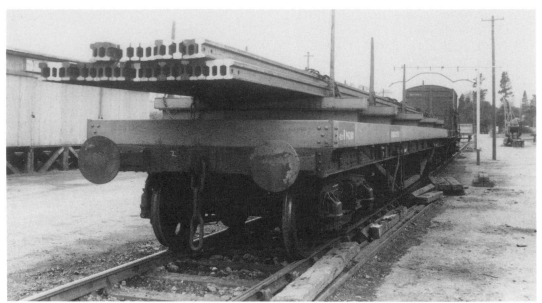

A rare view within the yard itself, showing a bolster wagon loaded with rails. The photograph is looking back towards the station approach, with the goods shed on the left-hand side – the corrugated building is an addition on the goods shed platform and was presumably used as extra storage. No record has been found as to when it was provided. On the side of the actual goods shed was a conventional ground signal mounted at the driver's eye-level to assist with sighting.

British Railways

No. 5092 *Tresco Abbey* at the head of an up express from South Wales on the through line at the station, 20.9.1955.

R.C. Riley

A grey day at Chipping Sodbury in the early 1950s and only a few passengers are awaiting the arrival of the up stopping service. This was one of five passenger services that served the station each way daily.

L.G.R.P.

Another Arnold vehicle photographed in 1948, after the company had been absorbed by B.Q.C. The wagon is standing on the new sidings at Chipping Sodbury where the end of the weighing machine office is also visible on the extreme right. The amount of mineral traffic can be gauged, rising from 5,534 tons in 1903 to 53,410 tons in 1925 and 69,225 tons in 1927. Output reached its peak in 1931 when 87,680 tons of aggregate was despatched.

L.G.R.P.

A more modern type of vehicle having 20-ton capacity compared with the 12-tons of most of the earlier wooden-bodied wagons. From 1928 to 1938 Arnolds' operated a 2ft. gauge railway within the quarry which was used to convey overburden from the quarry to a waste tip. Two 4-wheeled internal combustion machines (one diesel mechanical and the other petrol mechanical) were used.

Author's Collection

COALPIT HEATH

This was the penultimate station on the new line and the last of the four-track layouts. As the name implies the station was located in an area dotted with coal workings with the result that coal constituted the major traffic.

From the east the station was approached on a gently sweeping curve and passed over a bridge that carried a colliery line at right angles to the main route. A little further on was a spindly girder bridge carrying a footpath over the line. The colliery line connected Mayshill Colliery with the Midland Railway route from Mangotsfield to Yate. After the girder bridge came a small goods yard on the down side and the passenger station was immediately afterwards. The main station buildings were also on the down side of the line.

Access to the station for both vehicles and pedestrians was from the nearby Ram Hill, (the more appropriately named Station Road was some distance away!) it then joined the Bristol to Coalpit Heath road a little way to the west. The actual private road to the railway led to the rear of the down side buildings and by turning sharp right

Looking east through the station *c.* 1930 with a distant view of the girder bridge carrying the footpath over the line. The colliery sidings are beyond the station on the left-hand side and can be seen to have a train of wagons standing in them. The building on the up side was unique to the railway although the same type of canopy and roof design was used at several other locations including Lambourn.

Mowat Collection

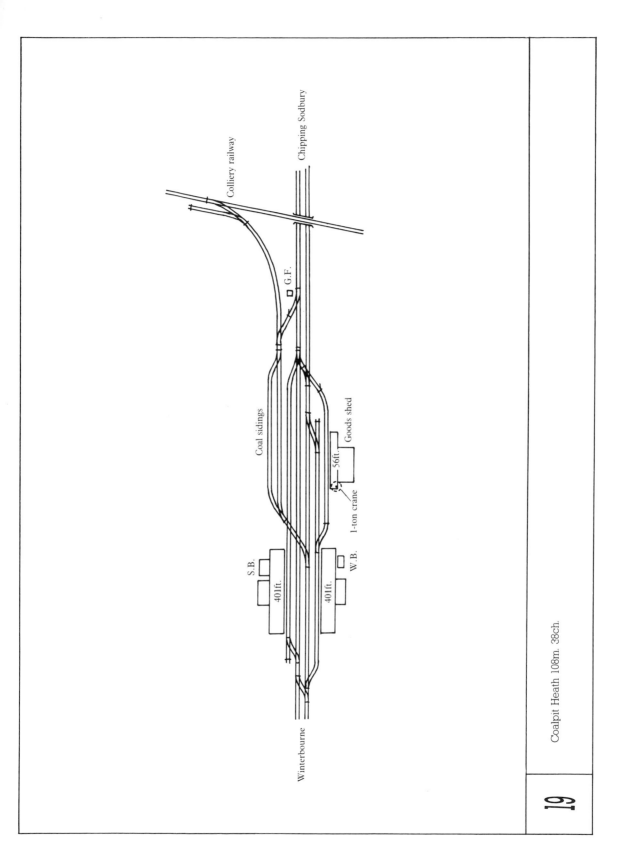

Colliery railway

Chipping Sodbury

G.F.

Coal sidings

Goods shed

56ft.

1-ton crane

S.B.

401ft.

W.B.

401ft.

Winterbourne

Coalpit Heath 108m. 38ch.

19

continued on towards the goods yard. A 15-ton capacity cart weighbridge was provided within the yard.

Despite the four-track layout previously referred to, the original layout here was slightly different from the other stations, with up and down running loops together with a single goods mileage loop, alongside which was a small goods lock-up and loading platform. The mileage loop could accommodate twenty four-wheeled vehicles whilst the actual layout can be discerned from the accompanying track plan. Although the passenger station opened at the same time as the other stations on the new line, public goods facilities were not available until 17.8.1904.

On the up side passenger platform was a small brick-built waiting shelter and toilet, both platforms were connected by a roofed metal footbridge, No. 289B from Paddington, which had a span of 79ft. 8in. and height from rail level of 16ft. 2in. The up side building was unique on the line in that its canopy extended back as part of the actual roof. In itself this was a common feature of many small station buildings erected on the GWR around this time, although why it was provided here in place of the more usual design used on the route is unclear – the cost of the up side building was identical to that at most of the other stations. Due to the curvature of the line, the signalbox was positioned on the up side and to the rear of the actual platform to ensure good visibility. The 'box itself was of brick and to the same design as that at Chipping Sodbury. Its size was 33ft. 6in. x 13ft. x 9ft. 6in. to the floor. Official records show that when originally opened a 33-lever frame was installed but with an unrecorded type of locking. By July 1908 this was altered to a 47-lever frame with horizontal

From the vantage point of the girder bridge and looking back towards the station. The goods siding with lock-up and access road show up well. On the up main line No. 6601 is at the head of a long freight, probably bound for the yards at Swindon. 20.9.1955.

R.C. Riley

tappet 3-bar locking, both frames known to have been spaced with the levers at 5in. centres. A block-switch was also provided. To the rear of the signalbox was a small ash bin and there was a lamp room and coal store at the London end of the up platform. All the buildings at the station were converted to electric lighting in early 1939 at a reported cost of £185.

At first glance such a rapid change in facilities may appear slightly strange, but it is likely to have been due to an agreement signed on 8.10.1903 between the GWR and Dame Emily Francis Smith and Charles Edward Hungerford Atholl Colston who operated the Coalpit Heath Colliery Company.[1] The aforementioned individuals were the owners of a coal mine nearby and the agreement drawn up was to provide two new loop sidings on the north side of the running lines with trailing connections into the main lines. Each of these new loop sidings could accommodate 15 wagons, and a connection was also made into the previously mentioned colliery line. Access to the main line was via a trailing connection at either end – this can be seen from the accompanying track plan. A ground frame of 4 levers which were bolted from the signalbox controlled the exit from the loops into the up main line at the west end of the station. It followed then that a number of additions and alterations to the signalling were necessary as a consequence of the new arrangements and which included new ground disc signals as well as repositioning of the up platform line starting signal. The cost of the new works was borne by Smith and Colston and although a date for the introduction of the new facilities is not available, it is likely to have been around July 1908. A gate separated the colliery sidings from the colliery line itself.

A set of instructions as to the working of the sidings was contained in the GWR Sectional Appendix:

Siding Connection and Ground Cabin

A Siding Connection on the Up Line side is worked by a Ground frame, and situated about 350 yards on the Swindon side of the Station Signal Box, for the purpose of working traffic to and from the Colliery Sidings and Lines.

---

1. Although not directly related to the story of Coalpit Heath station it maybe of interest to briefly refer to the history of the actual colliery. The name 'Coalpit Heath Coal Co.' (Ltd. from 1900 to 1926) collectively applied to three collieries, Froglane, Mayshill and Nibley which are known to have been producing coal prior to 1832. A mile-long branch from the MR to the workings was provided in 1846.

At least five private locomotives are known to have worked the colliery lines as follows:

	0-4-0T	Built by Fletcher Jennings in 1866
	0-6-0ST	Built by Fox Walker in 1876.
Lord Roberts	0-6-0ST	Built by Peckett in 1900.
Lord Salisbury	0-6-0ST	Built by Peckett in 1906.

4-wheel diesel mechanical, built by Ruston Hornsby in 1946.

There is no record that any of these engines were registered to work over GWR metals at Coalpit Heath station for shunting or access purposes. Similarly it is not known if any private owner wagons existed.

Another freight and this time 'Austerity' 2-8-0, No. 90448 on a down mixed working about to enter the station. On the extreme left the remains of the colliery sidings can be seen, with the ground sloping away to the connection with the former colliery line.

R.C. Riley

The points are worked from the Ground Frame and controlled from the Station signal Box.

Telephone communication is provided between the Station Signal Box and the Ground Frame, and a clear understanding between the Signalman and the man appointed to work the Ground Frame must be made before shunting operations are performed.

If the Main Line is occupied by the working, the man at the Ground Cabin must take immediate steps to clear the Line when requested to do so by the Signalman at the Station Box, and the latter must have the assurance of the Groundsman that the Line is clear before he allows any Up Train or Engine to come forward.

The Key to the Ground Cabin must be kept in the Signal Box when not in use, and the Porter appointed to work the Siding must return it to the Signal Box after the work has been finished.

Returning to the station proper, this was administered by a class 4 station master (originally class 2, but re-graded by 1934), two class 2 porters and three class 4 signalmen. The first two named groups received wages of 37s. 6d. and 18s. respectively per week in August 1914. The porters also acted as shunters when required. A house for the station master was provided on the down side of the line between the end of the platform and start of the goods yard. Water for both the station and house was provided originally from a well. At sometime between 1934 and 1938 the station master assumed control of neighbouring Winterbourne, an arrangement that continued for the rest of the life of the stations concerned.

Passenger traffic was sparse from the outset – indeed in the first eleven months of 1946 just 907 passengers used the station, with similarly small receipts for parcels and other miscellaneous items which were included with the passenger accounts. General goods traffic was likewise minimal. However, it was to be expected that coal output would account for most of the station's revenue with quantities of timber for use as pit props also being received at the station. As previously mentioned, the colliery was also provided with access to the Midland main line but it is not known how much traffic was dealt with by this means. Smaller amounts of other merchandise, mainly produce, were also received and forwarded.

A 'Britannia' No. 70024 *Vulcan* at the head of the thirteen coach 'Red Dragon' express from Carmarthen to Paddington. In the background the smoke-darkened panels of the footbridge show up well and are in stark contrast to those where the paint remains relatively unmarked.

R.C. Riley

Few other changes were reported at the station although on 12.10.1916 approval was given for a repositioning of the up distant signal and provision of a detonator placing machine. The cost of both is reported as £54. The track layout remained basically unaltered until January 1930 when the access to the goods loop was modified by substituting a facing turnout for the trailing connection into the up main. At the same time a change was made to the facing access into the down loop.

For most of the life of the station five stopping passenger services were provided each way daily, but by the early 1950s there was no Sunday service. Wagons to and from the colliery sidings were dealt with by two pick-up goods services, one in each direction. Besides the trains the area was also served by a number of 'bus services, these are detailed in the Chipping Sodbury station section. During World War II the station handled a number of ambulance trains with wounded American servicemen bound for nearby Frenchay Hospital.

The coal traffic gradually diminished until late 1951 when notice was given by the then owners, the National Coal Board, to terminate the siding agreement. The sidings and connection were removed at varying dates between 1953 and 1956.

WINTERBOURNE

This was the last of the stations on the new line which also had the basic two-track layout previously encountered at Brinkworth and Hullavington. The station served the village from which its name was derived and at the time of opening there were hopes that the area would develop as a residential centre within easy reach of Bristol, but this unfortunately failed to materialise until some time after the closure of the station.

Aside from the up and down main lines there was a small goods yard just west of the station on the up side of the line. Here were two loop sidings, one used as a mileage loop and the other facing a goods shed extending over one track width and containing a 43ft. loading platform and 50cwt. crane. The goods shed building is particularly interesting as apart from Chipping Sodbury this was the only station to boast what was normally a standard provision. The estimated cost of the 'shed was £845 4*s*. 4*d*. Two

A view towards Bristol around the time of opening. The alternate masonry and timber construction for the platform is clearly visible as are the number of persons in the photograph, most of whom appear to be railway staff. Beyond the footbridge the signalbox is just visible with the yard opposite. Notice also the gate on the down platform which afforded direct access to the station for the purpose of loading and unloading.

Science Museum/Pearson Collection

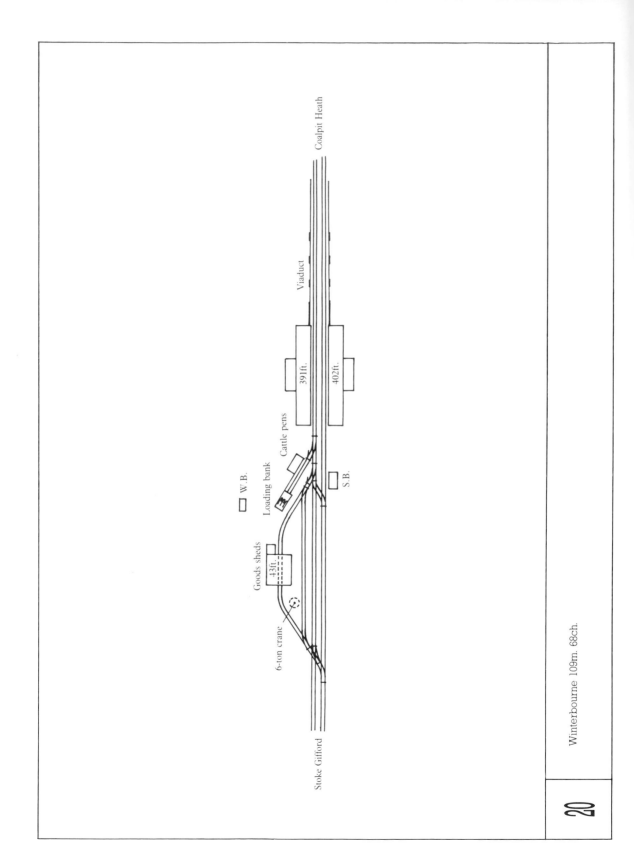

Stoke Gifford

6-ton crane

Goods sheds

43ft.

W.B.

Loading bank

Cattle pens

S.B.

391ft.

402ft.

Viaduct

Coalpit Heath

Winterbourne 109m. 68ch.

20

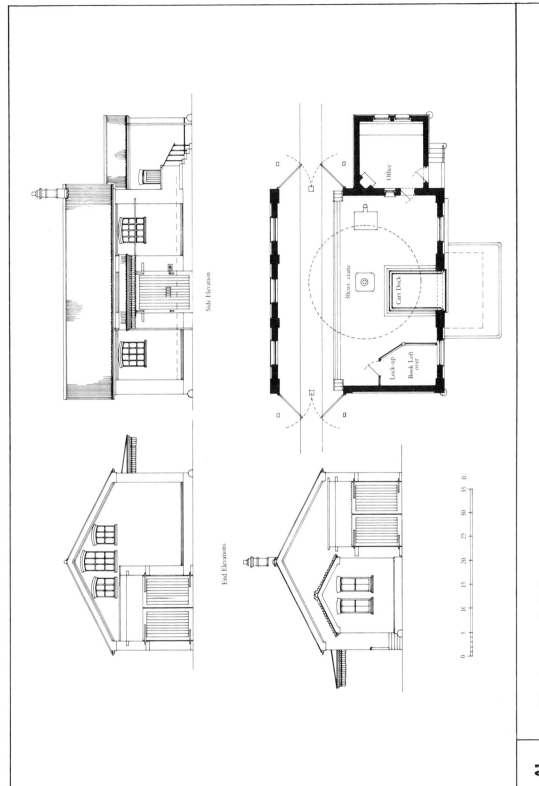

Side Elevation

End Elevations

30cwt. crane

Cart Dock

Office

Lock-up

Book Loft
over

0 5 10 15 20 25 30 35 ft.

Winterbourne goods shed.

21

wagons could be accommodated under cover within the shed and there was a small lean-to goods office at the London end of the building. Access to the goods sidings was via a trailing connection at either end whilst the track layout also included a crossover and single slip to facilitate ease of shunting. Catch points at either end protected the main lines from the goods siding.

Completing the track layout was a short siding directly at the west end of the up platform and this afforded access to some cattle pens and an end loading dock. This could accommodate just three vehicles and was again protected from the running line by a catch point.

The station buildings were similar in appearance to those encountered elsewhere and here the main structure on the down side was supported on deeply sunk arches. These extra footings are reflected in the cost of the building, £653 6s. 4d. compared with its neighbour at Coalpit Heath which was charged at £491 17s. 7d. On the opposite platform the waiting shelter was identical to those at Hullavington, Little Somerford and Brinkworth although at Winterbourne the building was costed at £172 11s. 6d., some 1s. 6d. more than its neighbours.

At the Bristol end of the station a plate girder bridge crossing the railway was supported on brick piers. This carried the Winterbourne Down to Watley's End road over the railway from which access was available to the station site. To reach the passenger station a sweeping drive led down from the south of the railway to the rear of the down platform, 'Private Road' status being maintained by the existence of a gate and warning sign. No vehicle access was available to the up platform and instead a footbridge connected both up and down sides at the west end of the buildings. Water to the station was supplied from a well to the rear of the up platform.

To reach the yard a similar access road, although slightly wider, led down from the north of the road bridge, again there was a gate although for most of the time this remained permanently open. As with neighbouring Coalpit Heath, a 'Station Road' was some distance from the line.

The goods yard approach continued on past the cattle pens and end loading bank, past a weighbridge (12-ton capacity) and hut and on to the rear of the goods shed. A further fixed yard crane, this time of 6-ton capacity and positioned between the two goods sidings just west of the goods shed completed the original facilities.

Controlling the layout was a brick-built signalbox on the down side of the line which was positioned just opposite the cattle pens. It measured 25ft. x 12ft. x 9ft. to the operating floor and contained a double twist lever frame of 27 levers set at 5in. centres. A block switch was also provided. Nearby was a small ash bin and coal store for both the station buildings and signalbox.

Traffic at the station was small although an amount of mineral traffic was forwarded which up to 1930 accounted for a large part of the receipts. Unfortunately it has not been possible to discover the exact nature of this traffic. There is another anomaly concerning the passenger traffic, for a glance at the traffic statistics (Appendix B) reveals that the number of tickets issued dropped dramatically after 1913, a feature in common with Coalpit Heath and Chipping Sodbury; again the reason for this is not clear but the most likely being the outbreak of war. Probably the most consistent

Looking in the same direction some fifty years later. The timber half platforms' can be seen to have been superseded by stone facing, a common feature at many Western Region locations during the early 1950s.

Colin Maggs

traffic was that of coal received although the records show that an amount of livestock was also handled.

When opened the station originally came under the control of a grade 2 station master and Mr W. Andrews is believed to have been the first postholder. He was succeeded around March 1911 by Mr W.J. Glasson who was transferred from a similar position at Wrington. It is not certain if at this stage a company house was provided to accompany the post as official records state that approval for a station masters' house was not given until the end of the following year, 1912, the construction contract being awarded to S. Robertson, of Bristol in May 1913.

Despite the canvassing efforts of both the local staff as well as the District Office at Bristol the station never really recovered from its decline after 1913 and this is reflected in the numbers of staff employed, from eight at the time of opening in 1903 to just three in 1931. Of these one was the signalman (the 'box was open on a 'half-day' basis only, i.e. 6.30 a.m. to 2.30 p.m. and closed in the afternoons, at night and at weekends) and two were grade 1 porters who alternated between early and late turn duties. Surprisingly a station master post was still officially allocated although the position was then vacant and the station did not officially come under the control of neighbouring Coalpit Heath until sometime after 1934.

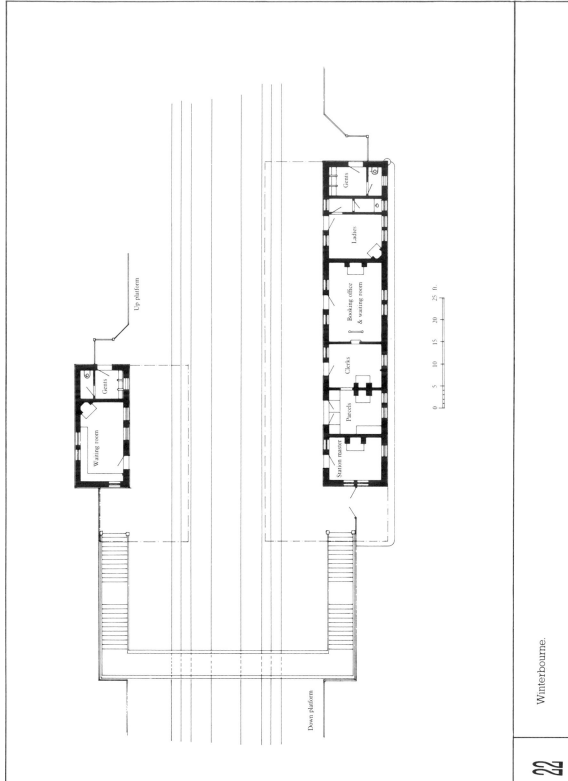

Up platform

Waiting room

Gents

Gents

Ladies

Booking office
& waiting room

Clerks

Parcels

Station master

Down platform

0   5   10   15   20   25 ft.

Winterbourne.

22

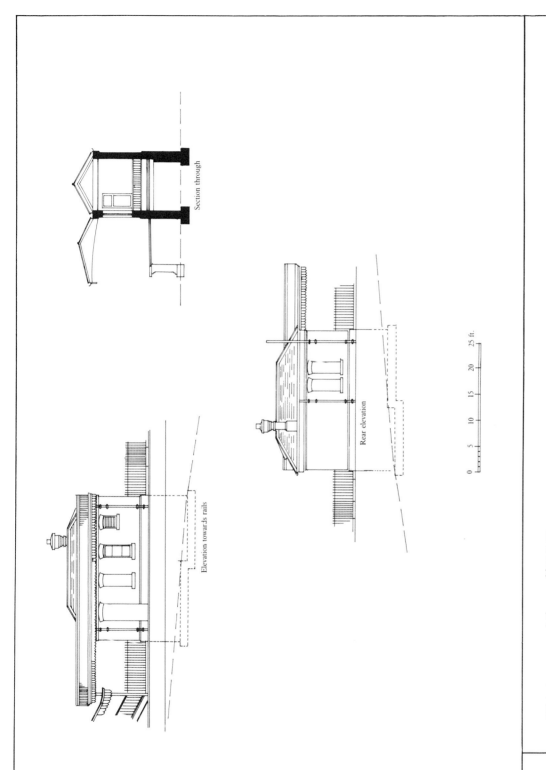

Section through

Elevation towards rails

Rear elevation

0   5   10   15   20   25 ft.

Winterbourne up platform waiting room.

23

SHUNTING OPERATIONS AT LITTLE SOMERFORD, HULLAVINGTON, BADMINTON, CHIPPING SODBURY, COALPIT HEATH, AND WINTERBOURNE.

The main lines at these Stations are on Gradients, as shewn below, and the greatest possible care must be exercised by each member of the Staff in carrying on shunting operations:—

STATION.		GRADIENT.				FALLING TOWARDS.
Little Somerford	....	.... 1 in 400	....	....	....	Brinkworth,
Hullavington	....	.... 1 in 300	....	....	....	Little Somerford.
Badminton	....	.... 1 in 300	....	....	....	Chipping Sodbury.
Chipping Sodbury	,...	.... 1 in 300	....	....	....	Stoke Gifford.
Coalpit Heath	....	.... 1 in 300	....	....	....	Stoke Gifford.
Winterbourne	....	,... 1 in 300	....	....	....	Stoke Gifford.

The following arrangements must be adopted at each Station:—

PASSENGER VEHICLES WITH HAND BRAKES.

In all cases whenever possible, and when the work can be carried out without seriously delaying the train, such vehicles must be shunted into a siding by the train from which they are detached.

When it is necessary to detach such vehicles at the Platform, or at any other point on the Main Lines, the person who detaches them must, before doing so, properly secure them by means of the hand brakes with which they are fitted, unless an engine is previously coupled on to the rear of the vehicles.

When the vehicles are removed a competent man must accompany them, ready to apply the brake at any time and prevent them getting beyond control, and when the vehicles are safely placed in a siding the brakes must be applied so as to prevent them moving.

PASSENGER VEHICLES WITHOUT HAND BRAKES.

Vehicles without hand brakes must be placed in a siding by the train from which they are detached, unless such cannot be done without causing serious delay to the train. In such cases, under the personal authority and supervision of the Station Master, the vehicles may be detached from the train, but before this is done a competent man must secure each one by means of hand scotches placed under the wheels, and also a brake stick placed through the wheel gear of one wheel ready to use as a brake, and he must remain with the vehicles until they are safely placed in a siding and locked in.

When it is necessary to remove such vehicles, otherwise than by an engine attached, two competent men must always be with the vehicles while moving—one with hand scotches and the other with a brake stick placed through the wheel gear—and they will be held responsible for using such appliances, so as to prevent the possibility of the vehicles getting beyond control. The moving of the vehicles must be carried out at a very slow speed.

SHUNTING OF VEHICLES DURING HEAVY WINDS AND STORMS.

In all cases vehicles, with or without brakes, must be placed in a siding by the train from which they are detached and not left on the Main Line.

SHUNTING OF FREIGHT WAGONS.

Shunting of wagons without an engine being attached and a competent person in charge of brakes *is strictly forbidden*.

The Station Master is responsible for seeing that these instructions are strictly carried out and that each member of the Staff has been made fully acquainted with them; also that a brake stick and two hand scotches are always kept at each end of each Platform for immediate use if required.

Reproduced from the GWR Sectional Appendix.

FOUR

ALONG THE LINE – OVER THE YEARS

*Even if strength fail, boldness at least
will deserve praise: in great endeavours
even to have had the will is enough.*

Propertius

At the same time as work was being completed on the Badminton line, Pearson's were also involved in the doubling of the former B & SWU line through Patchway. This resulted in the famous twin-bore tunnels on different levels, a permanent reminder of the changes brought about by the re-vamping of the former B & SWU line into an integral part of the new main line to Wales.

The Badminton line itself terminated at Filton Junction and so trains to and from Wales would use the former branch before continuing on through the Severn tunnel. In this way there would be a considerable saving on mileage compared with the previous route via Gloucester and a further useful saving in avoiding the congestion around Bristol. The GWR were no doubt interested to see just how much traffic was being routed via the new line and a census was carried out. This record has survived in the form of an official Locomotive, Carriage and Wagon Dept. document of 1904 and it provides a unique record of the number of trains run – the comparison between the original main line and Badminton route being especially clear:

Traffic West of Wootton Bassett

Statement showing the estimated number of Great Western Railway Company's Passenger and Goods Trains run between the undermentioned Stations and Junctions during the Year ended 30th. June 1904, based on the actual number of trains run during the months of September 1903 and January 1904.

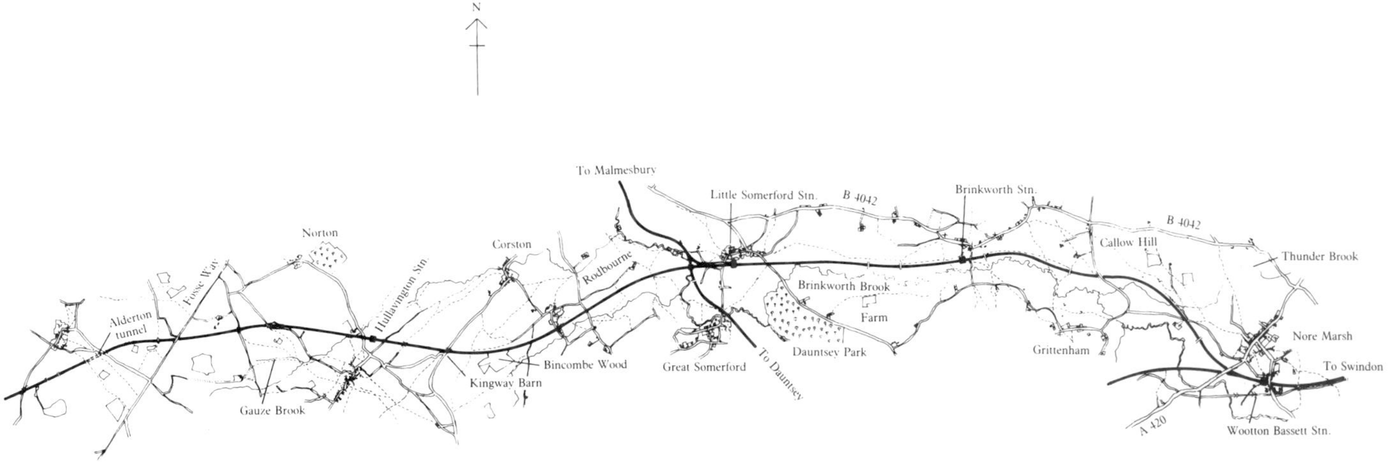

The Badminton line – its route through the southern fringes of the Cotswolds.

Thunder Brook
Nore Marsh
To Swindon
Wootton Bassett Stn.
A 420
B 4042
Callow Hill
Grittenham
Brinkworth Stn.
Little Somerford Stn.
B 4042
Brinkworth Brook
Farm
Dauntsey Park
To Dauntsey
Great Somerford
To Malmesbury
Rodbourne
Bincombe Wood
Corston
Kingway Barn
Hullavington Stn.
Norton
Gauze Brook
Fosse Way
Alderton Tunnel

N

Wootton Bassett junction seen looking east from the road bridges over the Bristol and Badminton lines in 1921. In the foreground is the West signalbox, with an interesting train of four-wheeled passenger stock in the down sidings. On the extreme right is the stacking ground referred to in the stations section.

L.G.R.P.

Between		Passenger trains	Goods trains	Total trains
Wootton Bassett	South Wales Direct Jc	29-544	18-102	47-646
S. Wales Direct Jc	Brinkworth	7-218	5-598	12-816
Brinkworth	Little Somerford	7-218	5-584	12-802
Little Somerford	Hullavington	7-218	5-584	12-802
Hullavington	Badminton	7-218	5-584	12-802
Badminton	Chipping Sodbury	7-158	5-584	12-742
Chipping Sodbury	Westerleigh East Jc	7-806	5-584	13-390
Westerleigh E. Jc	Junction with Mid. Rly	–	–	–
Junction with MR	Westerleigh W. Jc	–	–	–
Westerleigh E. Jc	Westerleigh W. Jc	7-806	5-584	13-390
Westerleigh W. Jc	Coalpit Heath	7-806	5-584	13-390
Coalpit Heath	Winterbourne	7-806	5-584	13-390
Winterbourne	Stoke Gifford Goods Yd	7-806	5-584	13-390
Stoke Gifford G.Y.	Stoke Gifford Jc	7-846	5-934	13-782

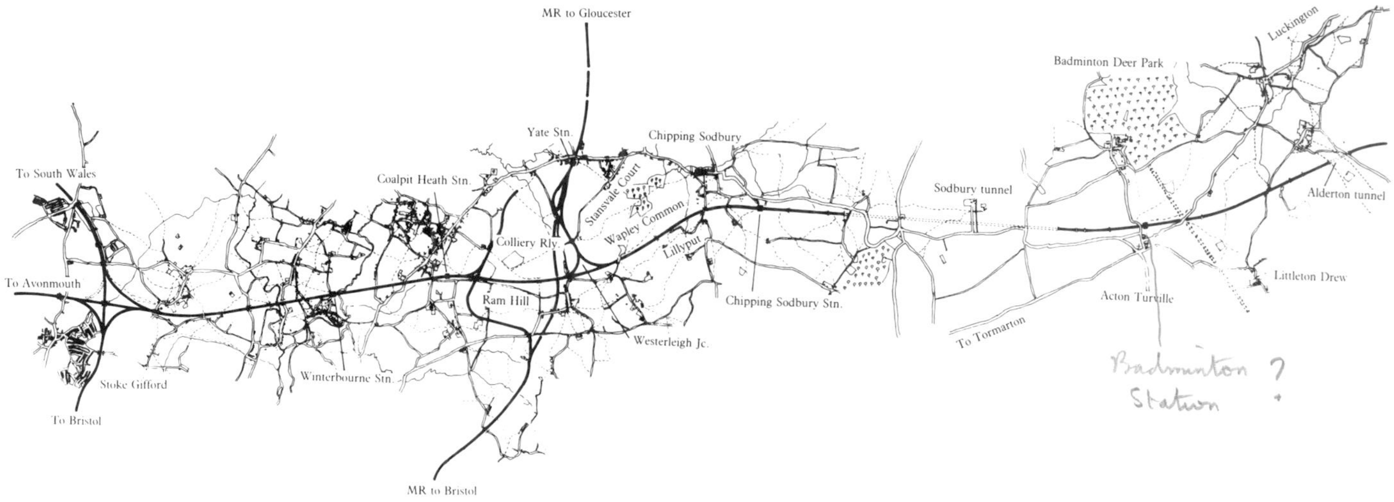

The Badminton line – its route through the southern fringes of the Cotswolds.

Luckington

Alderton tunnel

Littleton Drew

Badminton Deer Park

Acton Turville

Badminton ?
Station :

To Tormarton

Sodbury tunnel

Chipping Sodbury

Chipping Sodbury Stn.

MR to Gloucester

Westerleigh Jc.

Wapley Common

Lilliput

Stanshawe Court

Yate Stn.

Coalpit Heath Stn.

Colliery Rly.

Ram Hill

MR to Bristol

Winterbourne Stn.

To South Wales

To Avonmouth

Stoke Gifford

To Bristol

Again from the road bridge but this time with the Badminton line prominent. Besides the main line there are two up and one down goods loops, all of the latter being classified for permissive working. Note also the path leading to the signalbox from the bridge, down the bank and along the cess. It would appear this was the official walking route to the 'box.

L.G.R.P.

Stoke Gifford Jc	Patchway Jc	3-042	3-858	6-900
Stoke Gifford Jc	Filton Branch Stn	4-806	2-076	6-882
Filton Branch Stn	Filton Branch Jc	4-806	2-076	6-882
S.Wales Direct Jc	Dauntsey	22-326	12-504	34-830

The table raises some interesting point, not least of which is that at its least busy point, viz Badminton to Chipping Sodbury, some 12,742 services ran, equal to 35 services daily. Note also how the number of passenger trains increased dramatically after Chipping Sodbury, indicating a working from Bristol which terminated at the station. Also of interest are the other variations between stations and there is a marked drop between trains continuing to South Wales compared with those running to Bristol.

All this traffic would increase still further on the Badminton line when the connection with the MR was opened. This would connect the GWR line at Westerleigh (between Chipping Sodbury and Coalpit Heath) with the Midland Railway at Westerleigh just south of their station at Yate on their Bristol to Gloucester main line.

On the Badminton line just west of Wootton Bassett, the gentle slope of the cutting so typical of parts of the route. The engine is No. 3854 and is in typical drab wartime condition with the cab side window blanked out.

British Railways

Although originally authorised as part of the 1896 Act, and indeed as previously recounted already built, a dispute between the GWR and MR had precluded the use of the new connections. The consequent opening and closing dates for the loops and junctions were indications of the disagreements to follow:

1.5.1903	Westerleigh East and West loops opened for goods traffic.
26.6.1903	Inspection of main line by Col. Yorke. Loops not inspected as '. . . junction lines are not completed.'
1.7.1903–30.6.1904?	Junctions and connections disused.
4.2.1907	Lines again reported as taken out of use following dispute with MR.
9.3.1908	Lines re-opened for goods traffic.
20.10.1908	Inspection by Col. Yorke.
2.11.1908	First recorded use of new connections by GWR north–south express passenger services.

Two views of Callow Hill Bridge between Wootton Bassett and Brinkworth at 85m. 29ch. This was the site of subsidence in the autumn of 1946 and a number of cracks can be seen to have appeared in the road surface. A cure was affected by sinking concrete blocks into the cutting sides nearby to forstall further movement. (The present day M4 motorway now runs parallel with the railway south of the line and this particular bridge is clearly visible from the roadway.)

Both British Railways

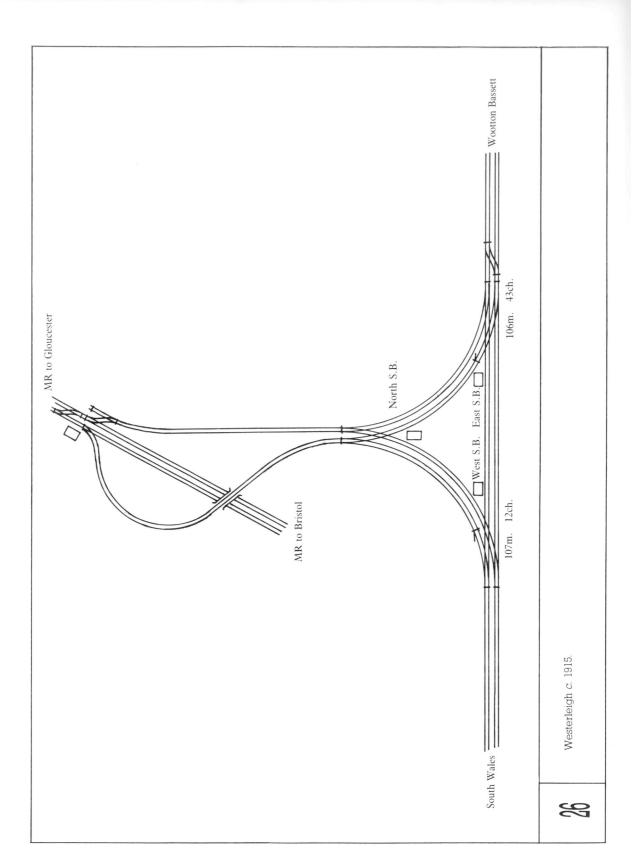

MR to Gloucester

MR to Bristol

North S.B.

West S.B. East S.B.

Wootton Bassett

106m. 43ch.

107m. 12ch.

South Wales

Westerleigh c. 1915.

26

(The signalboxes at Westerleigh East and Westerleigh North were closed between 4.2.1907 and 9.3.1908, although both remained intact. Westerleigh West was kept for use if required as a block post on the main line between Chipping Sodbury and Coalpit Heath. Block switches were provided in all the Westerleigh 'boxes. On the basis that the traffic survey above related to just two months it is likely that some goods traffic used the connections at intervals between 1.7.1903 and 4.2.1907.)

This dispute had arisen over matters totally unconnected with the Badminton line itself and instead were centred on the GWRs desire to develop a new direct service from Bristol to Birmingham. In consequence the GWR naturally proposed to route their trains from Bristol over their own lines, via Filton to Westerleigh and thence over the MR to Gloucester. Various other arrangements including the construction of a new GWR line from Cheltenham to Honeybourne would allow direct access to Birmingham via Stratford. The MR, however, objected to this, despite the fact that they already operated a very successful route from Bristol to Birmingham, and for their part stated that they would allow GWR traffic for the Midlands to run on their line through Mangotsfield. By doing so the MR would of course pick up considerable revenue. Understandably with their new route via Westerleigh now available the GWR refused. A further complication was a wish expressed by the GWR to afford

No. 7923 *Speke Hall* and an unidentified 'Castle' double-head a South Wales express between Wootton Bassett and Brinkworth in early BR days.

National Railway Museum/J.F. Russell Smith

access via Westerleigh, to the joint Severn & Wye line eleven miles north of Yate. (The original GWR Bill of 1896 had proposed an independent branch from Westerleigh to the Severn & Wye. This though was dropped due to opposition from the MR and the Yate junctions were substituted.)

For some time the result was stalemate during which time the GWR had submitted another Bill to Parliament for powers to build a line just over 1 mile long as a facing connection for trains from the direction of Yate straight to the Severn & Wye line. (This is clearly shown on the plan of running powers.) The GWR Bill received Royal Assent on 4.8.1905 as the 'GWR (Additional Powers) Act of 1905', and had the effect of waving a red flag to a bull as far as the MR were concerned. Consequently by early 1907 the Westerleigh connections were completely disused.

The GWR lost no time in starting the construction of the new Severn & Wye connection and despite the animosity that existed between both companies in relation to passenger working, an arrangement was reached whereby goods traffic could use both the Westerleigh curves and the new Berkeley loop from 9.3.1908.

The Badminton line was used a great deal for running in turns from Swindon works with the engines either taking a circular course via Bath and Filton or else turning on the triangle at Filton. Here No. 4081 *Glastonbury Abbey* is seen in superb external condition as it heads gently along near Brinkworth in the early 1950s. The cutting sides have had channels cut into them to assist drainage.

National Railway Museum/J.F. Russell Smith

Little Somerford looking east with the Malmesbury Branch connection on the left. Notice the two types of rail, bull head for the up and flat bottom on the down line.

British Railways

However, no agreement could be reached on the matter of passenger working and so in May 1908 the MR sought a legal judgement on the whole issue of Great Western through services. Their application was heard before Mr Justice Warrington who concluded that Great Western access to the MR at Yate could only be used for traffic to and from the Severn & Wye railway and not for any other purpose. The GWR appealed against the decision, and in October the Court of Appeal unanimously overturned the previous ruling. The way was thus clear for the new north–south expresses to run via Westerleigh, the only remaining requirement being a formal Board of Trade inspection.

Not wishing to loose any more time, on 16.10.1908 the GWR advised the Board of Trade that the new connections were ready for inspection and Col. Yorke visited the area just four days later on 20.10.1908. Verbal approval was given almost immediately although somewhat surprisingly it was not until the 19 November that the written report of inspection was available:

Little Somerford viaduct from the south with twelve arches each having a 25ft. span and one over the River Avon of 58ft. span. The view was taken in 1922 and in the foreground is the light trackwork of the Malmesbury branch with Great Somerford station a little way to the south of the photographer. The bridge carrying the main line over the branch can also be clearly seen. This was part of the branch abandoned in 1933 as a result of the new connection provided and yet it was still intact at this point as a siding until 1961.

L.G.R.P.

Sir, I have the honour etc, . . . I inspected on the 20th idem Rlys. Nos. 1a., 2a., and 3a. (known as Midland Junction Railways), authorised by the Great Western . . . These lines form a triangular junction between the S.Wales Direct line and the Midland Railway from Bristol to Gloucester.

Railway No.1a. is 1m. 34chs. in length, of which 60chs. is double, and 54chs. single line. The steepest gradient is 1 in 150, and the sharpest curve has a radius of 15.15chs. For the greater part of its length the line is carried on embankment, of which the greatest height is 38ft. There are two underbridges, one, having an opening of 35ft, with a brick arch, and the other, with an opening of 10ft, constructed with steel trough flooring. There are also two small culverts. All these works are in good condition, and the steel troughing under the line gave moderate deflections when tested. The permanent way is laid with rails weighing 77.5lbs. per yard and chairs weighing 35lbs. each, each chair being secured to the sleepers by two 7/8in., bolts. The sleepers are 9ft. by 10in. by 5in., and they are

During the 1940s the abandoned portion of the Malmesbury branch was utilised for stock storage and a long line of carriage underframes are visible. These were the remains of burnt out coaches following an air raid on Bristol. An amount of this stock was visible from the main line, and one of the more interesting vehicles is a London Metropolitan Line coach on the extreme left, although why this particular vehicle should be stored here is unclear.

British Railways

placed at varying distances apart, the greatest being 2ft. 6in. from centre to centre. The ballast consists of limestone and slag.

Rly. No. 2a. is 59chs in length, all single line, nearly the whole of which is carried on embankment, the greatest height being 18ft. The steepest gradient is 1 in 150, and the sharpest curve has a radius of 20chs. There are two underbridges, one, with a 10ft. opening on the square, is constructed with steel trough flooring, and the other, with an opening of 52ft on the square, is constructed with steel plate girders, cross girders, and rail bearers. There is also one small culvert. The works are in good condition, and the girders under the line gave moderate deflections when tested. The permanent way is similar in all respects to that of Rly. No. 1a.

Rly. No. 3a. is 37 chains in length, all double line, the whole of which is on embankment having a height of 31ft. The steepest gradient is 1 in 150, and the sharpest curve has a radius of 15.15chs. There are two small underbridges, each having a brick arch. Both these bridges are in good order, and there are no other works. The permanent way is similar in all respects to that of Rly. No.1a. There

The west end of Alderton tunnel with the various forms of strata clearly visible. This was the shorter of the two tunnels on the line, at 506yds. in length and was not ventilated.

L.G.R.P.

are no stations on these railways. The points and signals of the junction with the Midland Railway are worked from that Company's Yate Station signalbox. . . . The points and signals of the junction between Railways Nos. 1a. and 3a. are worked from Westerleigh North Box, which contains 14 levers in use and 6 spare levers. The points and signals of the two junctions between Rlys. 1a. & 3a. and the S.Wales Direct Railway are worked from Westerleigh East and West signalboxes, on the South Wales Direct Rly., which were inspected and reported on by me in June 1903. The interlocking being correct and the condition of lines satisfactory, I can recommend the Board of Trade to sanction the use of these railways for passenger traffic.

I have the honour, &c.

H.A. Yorke

Regular use was being made of the new connections for north–south through trains by the end of the year.

No. 5027 *Farleigh Castle* passes under bridge No. 270 just east of Badminton station with the up 'Red Dragon' express in 1953. The bracket signal controlled the entrance to the station and loop with the f.p.l. for the latter turnout which is visible under the bridge. Notice the sighting board for the down main home signal, necessary to give approaching fast trains a clear view of the signal's indication against what was a cluttered background.

G.F. Heiron

Of the passenger services using the Badminton line the principal amongst these were the express services to and from Fishguard. The Cunard liner RMS *Mauretania* arrived at Fishguard for the first time on 30.8.1909 and the GWR ran a special fast service over the 260mls. to Paddington via Badminton in 4hr. 36 min. The following day the daily newspapers were full of admiration for the new service; *The Daily Telegraph*, '. . . Despite the tremendous speed – more than sixty five miles an hour was attained at times, the running was perfectly smooth. There was not a single jolt from start to finish . . .', whilst the *Daily News* reporter in comparing previous trips stated, '. . . we shouldn't have reached Liverpool yet, and yet now we are in London. It is wonderful.'

In reality such achievements were the result of a special effort by all concerned to ensure a swift passage through customs as well as holding back other traffic to give the prestige trains a clear run. In addition there was the disadvantage that both passengers and baggage still had to be unloaded by tender, an unenviable occupation in inclement

<u>PRIVATE.</u>—For the use of the Company's Servants only.   NOTICE NO. 107.

GREAT WESTERN RAILWAY.

TIME TABLE OF THE JOURNEY

OF

THEIR MAJESTIES
THE KING AND QUEEN

AND SUITE,

FROM

AVONMOUTH DOCK SOUTH PIER TO BADMINTON

(*Via* PILNING JUNCTION)

AND FROM

BADMINTON TO PADDINGTON,

ON

FRIDAY, JULY 10th, 1908.

The Great Western Royal Train will be used, and it will run on the Main Line from Didcot East Junction to Paddington.

For Special Instructions to be observed in connection with the working of the Royal Train see fourth and fifth pages of this Notice. Also the following exceptions :—

With reference to paragraph (*a*) of Clause 11 in the Instructions on page 4, no Engine, Train or Vehicle must be allowed to cross or foul the line upon which the Royal Train will run between Old Oak Common East and Paddington Arrival Platform for at least 10 minutes before the passing of the Royal Train.

ENGINES AND TRAINS OF EMPTY COACHES BETWEEN PADDINGTON AND WEST LONDON, AND PADDINGTON AND OLD OAK COMMON DEPÔTS.

With reference to the Instructions contained in paragraph (*d*) of Clause 11 and paragraph (*a*) of Clause 12, Up and Down Trains of empty coaches and engines between Paddington and West London, and between Paddington and Old Oak Common, may be treated as Passenger Trains and worked in accordance with paragraph (*c*) of Clause 12.

Tunnels.—Referring to Clause 25, page 5 of this Notice, Special instructions will be issued by the Bristol Divisional Superintendent respecting the examination and protection of the Patchway, Chipping Sodbury and Alderton Tunnels in connection with the passage of the Royal Train, and these must be strictly adhered to. The engine head lamps must be lighted before leaving Avonmouth Dock South Pier for Badminton, and again before leaving Badminton for Paddington.

Avonmouth Dock.—The single line between Avonmouth Dock South Pier and Gloucester Road is the property of the Bristol Corporation, and the Train will be under the control of their Docks Committee between those points.

Pilning and Avonmouth Line.—This is a single line from Gloucester Road, Avonmouth to Pilning Junction. Between Gloucester Road, Holesmouth Junction and Pilning Low Level, it is worked by Electric Train Staff; and between Pilning Low Level and Pilning Junction by Wooden Train Staff. The standard instructions for working a single line with Electric Train Staff and with Train Staff and Ticket must be observed over the sections of line to which those instructions apply respectively. The Special instructions shown on pages 4 and 5 of this Notice will also apply between Gloucester Road and Pilning Junction.

(✠) The Midland and South Western Junction, London & North Western, North & South Western Junction, and District Railway Companies, will take steps to prevent any Train or Vehicle passing over their respective bridges during the time the Royal Train is passing underneath. Arrangements must be made to advise the staff on these bridges of the approach of the Royal Train.

☞ In cases where the supply of this notice is sent out direct by me, a special form of receipt, printed on pink paper, will accompany the notice, and this receipt must be carefully filled up and forwarded to me **BY NEXT TRAIN.** The envelopes containing the receipts must be marked outside "Receipt for Royal Train Notice," and Guards must be instructed to personally deliver these letters immediately on arrival at Paddington.

In cases where this notice is distributed locally, receipt must be acknowledged **without delay** to your Superior Officer.

J. MORRIS,
Superintendent of the Line.

July 8th, 1908.

WYMAN & SONS, Ltd., Printers, Fetter Lane, London, E.C., and Reading

A delightful view of a down goods service on the opposite side of Bridge No. 270 taking the main line. At the head is another 38xx series 2-8-0, No. 3845, the fireman of which is attempting to get the left-hand injector to function, July 1957. Under GWR and BR ownership no locomotive water supplies were available at Badminton station although Pearsons' had obtained supplies from an old coal mine nearby. This though was admitted to be '. . . not of good quality'.

G.F. Heiron

weather conditions. A similar restriction also existed at Plymouth. But despite these problems, on the surface at least, it did appear as if Wilkinson had been correct and for the moment all eyes were focussed on Fishguard – it was destined to be a short-lived period of glory.

Apart from having some of the most talked about trains of the period running over it, the Badminton line was already making its name in other respects. Records show that on 27.8.1908 Chuchward's solitary Pacific *The Great Bear* had successfully worked a 100-wagon train from Paddington to the yards at Stoke Gifford via Badminton, and at about the same time the big 28xx 2-8-0 class began to take similar loads of coal in the other direction. The advantage of the new route was now obvious for with its gentle curves and easy gradients compared with the original line around Bath it was possible to economise on operating costs by working such sizeable trains.

A dramatic view of No. 5032 *Usk Castle* east of Chipping Sodbury tunnel with a Pembroke Dock to Paddington express seen just passing under an aqueduct (No. 3b). Bridge No. 274 can be seen in the background and is one of the 'flying arch' types. On the right part of the cutting has had a retaining wall provided whilst on the left is the down distant signal for Badminton (positioned on the down side for sighting purposes) and a bin of chippings used by the permanent way gang for minor corrections to the rail level.

G.F. Heiron

The GWR publicity department were certainly not slow to capitalise on these new possibilities as can be seen in several well-known photographs of these mammoth trains, although none appear to have been taken on the new line.

Because of the length of these trains special instructions were issued to staff as to their working;

Long Freight Trains

Certain trains are authorised to take a load of 60 or more wagons between Stoke Gifford and Swindon (via Badminton) and vice versa. When it is necessary to shunt these trains, Up and Down, for other trains to pass this must as a rule only be done at the Stations where there are Platform Loop Lines or Refuge Sidings constructed to hold such trains, and except to avoid serious delay to more important trains they must be allowed to proceed to the next Station where there are Through Lines or suitable Refuge Sidings.

It is likely that the publicity department had also been behind the move to refer to an engine class as associated with the new line, a series of 4-4-0s built between 1891

Instructions for the Chipping Sodbury tunnel taken from the GWR Sectional Appendix.

At the east end of Chipping Sodbury tunnel the sheer sides of the cutting are retained by walls to a considerable height and were intended to prevent slipping of the sides. A 70xx series 'Castle' emerging into daylight from the darkness of the tunnel at the head of a Carmarthen to Paddington express.

G.F. Heiron

and 1901 and were jointly known as the 'Badminton' or 'Atbara' class, No. 4100 carrying the actual name *Badminton*.

As previously detailed, the Badminton line itself diverged from the original GWR just west of Wootton Bassett station, turning immediately northwest to pass underneath a three-arched brick bridge carrying the Cricklade road over the line. Apart from two very short sections at 1 in 660 and then 1 in 237, the line is downhill for some three miles westwards whilst immediately after the bridge is a section of shallow cutting. This was built on two distinct levels and is an early indication of the difficulties experienced with some of the earthworks.

The line then takes a straight course, to emerge from the cutting with open farmland on either side and with several drinking places for cattle hard by the railway fence. Just over half a mile from the junction another three-arched brick bridge crosses the route after which there is a gradual but distinct change to embankment, the line passing over a brick and girder skew bridge with the road from Grittenham to Wootton Bassett underneath. It was here on the north side of the line that the GWR were obliged to construct a new road parallel with the railway for the convenience of the original owner, Sir Henry Bruce Meux. The embankment continues as the railway

A ventilation shaft on top of Chipping Sodbury tunnel with the mound of excavated material nearby clearly visible against the height of the surrounding land. (These mounds and the relevant towers are easily seen from the B4040 road and when seen at close quarters are of truely massive proportions. Most still retain their inherent characteristics as spoil heaps with the underground course of the railway easy to discern from their position.) As recounted earlier this was a 'wet' tunnel with an average of 500,000galls of water carried away daily by the culvert underneath the rails. (This increased to over 750,000galls in wet weather.) Not surprisingly the GWR investigated the possibility of using some of this water for their own purposes, one idea being to pipe it to the works at Swindon, this was however later ruled out because of the distance and gradients involved. Another possibility came with approaches received from the Midland Railway, Gloucester Water Company and Bath Corporation, it is not clear from the minutes if any of these options were later taken up.

British Railways

Private and not for Publication. Notice No. 2042.

GREAT WESTERN RAILWAY.

RESTRICTION OF SPEED

BETWEEN

South Wales and Bristol Direct Line.

UP LINE

BETWEEN

BADMINTON

AND

HULLAVINGTON

96 miles 40 chains and 94 miles 60 chains.

Repairs to permanent way. Commencing at once and until further notice the speed of all trains must not exceed 15 miles per hour when passing between the above-mentioned points.

Hullavington Up Distant Signal will be disconnected.

Warning Boards at 97 m. 20 ch.

This amends the restriction of speed of 15 miles per hour over the Up Line between Badminton and Hullavington shewn in Notices Nos. 2024 and 2025.

ACKNOWLEDGE RECEIPT.

R. G. POLE,
  Divisional Superintendent.
Bristol, December, 1940.

F. R. POTTER,
  Superintendent of the Line.

(2,500 6 × 5".)

The west end of Chipping Sodbury tunnel with a number of the buildings at Old Sodbury village above the portal. Of interest is the semicircular tunnel construction intended to give greater strength compared with a half-cirle. The face was constructed of masonry hewn from the nearby cutting and there is a lamp room visible adjacent to the up line. The view is taken some years after the line opened and it is known that during construction a trailing crossover existed just outside the tunnel although this was removed prior to the public opening.

L.G.R.P.

passes over a culvert which carries the deceptively named Thunder Brook under the line; after this comes a small girder bridge so affording access to farm land on either side.

Gradually the embankment peters out and is replaced by cutting near to where the present day M4 motorway passes over the route. Continuing on the railway what would at first seem to be a sharp curve to the west appears, although it should be remembered that nowhere on the main running lines is there any radius less than 1m. The curve continues on an embankment before giving way to cutting with another brick and girder bridge over the railway carrying the public road to Callow Hill village just to the north. This bridge caused the engineers considerable trouble in 1946 when the instability of the adjacent cuttings resulted in cracks in both the wing walls and road surface. A remedy was effected by sinking concrete shafts into the cutting sides to prevent further movement. Unfortunately the depth of the earthworks at this point prevents rail passengers from glimpsing views of Callow Hill village and the numerous nearby farms. Instead the cutting continues for some little while, its end marked by a three-arch bridge accessible from a stile on either side.

No. 70029 *Shooting Star* about to enter Chipping Sodbury tunnel with the 8.00 a.m. Neyland to Paddington service (due in London at 3.10 p.m.) in the spring of 1954. In the background is bridge No. 275 which carries a gated footpath over the line. The signal is Chipping Sodbury down distant with part of the bridge brickwork painted white as a sighting panel.

G.F. Heiron

There is now a sudden change to embankment, its edges again supported at intervals by deep sunken piles in an effect to achieve stability. Nearby a bridge allows the passage of a public footpath beneath the railway, one of several walkways in the vicinity.

The gradient now changes to a short section of level line at which point another waterway, this time a tributary of Brinkworth Brook passes beneath. This is followed by an occupation bridge under the line after which the slow descent at 1 in 300 continues westwards towards the first station at Brinkworth. From the high vantage point of the railway embankment the first signs of habitation can be seen north of the line whilst to the south it is just possible to glimpse a few of the outbuildings of Manor Farm, about half a mile distant.

Such views, however, are cut short as plunging into a deep cutting another bridge

A striking view of No. 70024 *Vulcan* at the head of the westbound 'Capitals United Express' from Paddington to Cardiff on Chipping Sodbury troughs in May 1961. The troughs themselves were 1570ft. long on both the up and down lines and were placed on one of the few sections of level line along the whole route. Water supplies were obtained from the River Frome at the east end and an aqueduct and hydrants at the west end.

G.F. Heiron

passses overhead followed shortly afterwards by a wide girder bridge which immediately precedes the entry to Brinkworth station. Within the actual station area the land is almost level and an occupation road can be seen paralleling the line for some distance on the down side. A little further south Brinkworth Brook follows its meandering course and it will continue to mark the railway's passage west as far as Little Somerford before it turns due south to join the River Avon.

Following the station there is a brief section of level track before the embankment allowing for a view of Clifford's Farm on the left, immediately followed by a fruit orchard. Corresponding with this the railway gradient changes briefly to a 1 in 600 rise although the length of this is minimal before the gradient dips once more in favour of the westbound trains. On either side open farmland can once again be seen, with the railway traversing this by alternate shallow cuttings and embankments punctuated by two occupation bridges over the line.

On 30.6.1925 the 10.25 a.m. Bristol to Swindon stopping passenger service was in the charge of brand new No. 4083 *Abbotsbury Castle* attached to a small capacity tender. The train has just left Chipping Sodbury station and has a motley selection of vehicles in tow, typical of the local services of the period. The engine is likely to be on a running in turn.

H.G.W. Household

Just beyond the 88 m. post from Paddington the land begins to drop away, but the railway maintains its course on embankment. This is quickly followed by an occupation bridge under the line whilst alongside the up line the ground is flat and can easily be seen to be wide enough to take an additional pair of running lines if required. At the same time the embankment continues with another occupation bridge allowing a small culvert to feed into the nearby Brinkworth Brook.

The railway is now approaching Little Somerford and as far as up trains are concerned it is one of the fastest stretches of the line. The actual station is near to the bottom of a descent that has lasted almost 10mls. and brings the railway to the watershed of the Thames and Avon. It is small wonder that over the years legends have arisen of speed records near this point with at least one authenticated as 100 m.p.h. behind steam, the engine being No. 7018 *Drysllwyn Castle*. Although this maybe the only official 'ton' behind steam recorded on the Badminton line, there is evidence to suggest that this speed and even more was achieved on other occasions. As early as 1906 Swindon were using the route as far as Stoke Gifford for trials of new locomotives and stories suggest that No. 2903 *Lady of Lyons* was given a specially cleared road all the way from Chipping Sodbury to Wootton Bassett on a light engine

A light load of just 15 vehicles for brand new No. 5623 on an up goods just east of Chipping Sodbury, 10.7.1925. These were the only water troughs on the Badminton line although water columns existed at Stoke Gifford, Wapley Common, Chipping Sodbury, Little Somerford and Wootton Bassett.

H.G.W. Household

trial in the course of which it is said to have reached no less than 120 m.p.h. somewhere between Little Somerford and Hullavington. Personnal interpretations of such stories will surely depend upon one's view of the engineering prowess of Swindon.

As the railway nears Little Somerford station the embankment affords a good view of the public road from Dauntsey to Malmesbury as it crosses under the line at an acute angle. Hard by this is a pair of railwaymens' cottages, probably originally provided for members of the permanent way staff. Following the roadbridge the embankment continues with an orchard to the right and a view of Little Somerford village to the north, although as referred to in the station description this was for many years little more than a hamlet. Before entering the station the railway first passes over another occupation road and then the goods yard appears on the right. As with the passenger station area, this too was built on embankment and so out of necessity the goods lock-up was supported on deep piles. At the Bristol end of the platform the road linking Little Somerford with its neighbour Great Somerford passes under the railway, the village cemetery being close by the south side of the embankment. At this point the

On a glorious summer day, 'Brittania Pacific' No. 70028 *Royal Star* passes under Lillyput Road bridge and its adjacent aqueduct with a Pembroke Dock to Paddington express. Near this spot was the Lillyput Quarry used by Pearson's when constructing the railway. The cutting sides are of rock only in the immediate vicinity of the bridge itself.

G.F. Heiron

gradient changes from the 1 in 400 descent in favour of up trains which persists through the station to a short section of level line and still upon embankment.

North of the main line it is still possible even today to pick out the 1933 diversion of the Malmesbury branch towards the main line, whilst a short distance further on, at the 90m. post, the main line is carried over the original route of the Malmesbury to Dauntsey railway by a girder bridge which has a span of 14ft. With the two lines being in such close proximity at this point it remains a matter of debate why it took the GWR some thirty years to provide what would appear such an obvious diversion. Possibly

Rounding the curve just prior to the Lillyput Road bridge (No. 280), No. 6961 *Stedham Hall* is in charge of an eastbound fitted freight and is working well on the 1 in 300 climb. The train has just passed the 'up' distant signal with its fogman's hut nearby. In conditions of poor visibility a member of the permanent way gang would be seconded to remain at the signal placing a detonator on the track every time the signal was in the 'on' position. Notice also the aqueduct (No. 6 from Wootton Bassett), just visible in the background. May 1963.

G.F. Heiron

the answer lies in a type of traffic between the two original stations of the branch, but without commencing an in-depth study of the branch itself this must remain conjecture.

Passing over the branch line it is just possible to glimpse Great Somerford station, although this is soon lost from view as the embankment gives way to the first of the big viaducts, consisting of twelve arches of 25ft. span and one of 58ft. span. Under the last arch the River Avon flows on its meandering way from its source at Crow Down Springs high in the Cotswolds to where it eventually emerges at Christchurch on the south coast.

Immediately after the viaduct the railway begins a long climb of 1 in 300, still on

Another 'Castle' hauled express this time passing the wartime signalbox at Wapley Common on 17.7.1955. The design of the 'box here is best described as functional yet austere, the labour for its building likely to have been provided by foreign workers. Similar style structures were erected on a number of GWR lines around this time including the new Westerleigh East 'box just out of sight to the right of the photograph, the sizes however varied considerably according to individual requirements. Wapley Common measured 38ft. x 13ft. x 11ft. (to the operating floor), and contained a vertical tappet five-bar frame of 59 levers. On the right the various loops are clearly visible along with the two entrances to the Ministry of Works yard. Both of these had gates across the track. Supervision of the Wapley and Westerleigh areas was exercised by the station master at Chipping Sodbury. It is known that at least one shunter was employed by the railway at Wapley in the 1950s transport being provided by rail to bring him to his place of work. This was usually by means of an empty stock train which would make a brief pause at the sidings. In the 1954 working timetable only one goods service daily in either direction is shown as calling at the sidings being the same train that formed the pick-up goods for the various stations on the line.

G.F. Heiron

Class '9', No. 92241 on the west curve at Westerleigh with a petrol tanker train from the former
Midland Railway route at Yate and is about to join the Badminton route. In the right background it is
just possible to discern the course of the east curve, although this had been disused since early 1950.

G.F. Heiron

embankment and swinging gently south at the same time. At this point a number of
minor ditches exist on either side of the railway, some feeding cattle troughs whilst
others continue under the line via a succession of culverts. These were provided as a
man-made form of irrigation and were intended to carry water away from the railway
earthworks. At the 90m. post an occupation path crosses under the line with the
embankment widening out to allow space for four tracks once again. All the bridges up
to this point, however, are only wide enough for a double line of rails.

The wide embankment continues for a while as the course of the railway straightens
to pass over a minor occupation bridge, this is followed almost immediately by a
bridge carrying the Rodbourne to Startley road under the railway. The village of
Rodbourne itself is to the right, and in the distance it is just possible to discern the
buildings of neighbouring Corston village. With the line still being carried above the

Westerleigh West junction looking towards London. In the distance is Westerleigh West signalbox, the curve to the Midland route disappearing around to the left on embankment and Bridge Farm in the foreground. The MR main line runs from left to right under the GWR route just behind the 107¼ milepost.

C.G. Maggs

level of the surrounding land the railway curves slightly to the right over a footpath and passes the hamlet of Rodbourn Bottom on the south side. Yet another bridge soon follows but this time it is marked by a change to cutting resulting in a skew girder structure. The main thoroughfare from Malmesbury to Stanton St Quinton once ran above, but for many years this has been reduced to the status of a farmtrack. With the line still swinging gently right in the cutting it is just possible to glimpse the tops of trees of Bincombe Wood extending to either side of the route. A three-arch bridge then passes overhead again with a minor road above, following which the cutting subsides and is replaced once more by an embankment wide enough for four tracks.

The line now passes over one of the major roads of the district, the A429 from Chippenham to Malmesbury which due to the route taken by the railway had to be diverted slightly. Similarly over the years it has been necessary to increase the height clearance under the girders leading to a deceptive dip in the road surface, more than one driver being caught unawares. (Bridge No. 251.) It was in this area that the Kingsway Barn was to be found; some reports refer to a spelling of 'Kingway', and it was referred to at the time of construction as the point where large amounts of soil were tipped. Still on a wide embankment the line continues westwards over a footpath leading from Hullavington to Corston before sidings begin to come into view on either

Seen from the MR main line towards Mangotsfield and Bristol an up goods and the 3.05 p.m. Paddington to Bristol passenger service cross at Westerleigh on 21.4.1960. At the time the Badminton line was under construction the Midland are reputed to have considered the area of Westerleigh as the site for a locomotive depôt though nothing came of this proposal.

C.G. Maggs

side of the line. This is the eastern extremity of Hullavington station which is marked by a further road underbridge, now a farm track, but once the public road from Marshfield to Malmesbury.

The amount of spoil deposited is quickly evident as the embankment extends for some distance on either side of the line, coming to an abrupt halt at the point where the Hullavington to Norton road passes under the railway at the west end of the station. Hullavington village itself is south of the line, but better views can be obtained to the north of Bradfield Farm with Gauze Brook passing nearby. This little waterway rises some miles west near the village of Littleton Drew and continues its wandering course for some distance before joining the Avon near to Little Somerford.

Mainly for the benefit of the farm a pathway runs under the railway, after which one of the major cuttings of the whole route commences which, with one minor exception, continues all the way to Alderton tunnel. Part way through the cutting the railway curves slightly left under an occupation bridge before resuming its straight path. Ahead now a 12in. water pipe is carried across the top of the cutting and this marks the course of the original Hullavington to Sherston road.

Somewhat surprisingly, in view of their vociferous opposition to the construction of other lines, much of the land needed for the railway at this point was purchased from

A 'Castle' hauled express near to Winterbourne in the mid-1930s. The scale of the earthworks at this point is readily visible and shows signs that an amount of hardcore has been added at some stage.

National Railway Museum/G.H. Soole

the Provost and College of Eton, the contract for which included the rights to mine for minerals should this ever be necessary. Although invisible from track level the Corston road was diverted to run parallel with the top of the cutting for a short distance before passing over the railway almost at right angles. The depth of cutting at this point is indicated by the fact that a bridge span of some 41ft. was required. Still in cutting the railway continues on, passing under Pig Lane bridge (No. 259) marking the point where the cutting begins to dip away and railway and land are level once again. After just 200yds. and coinciding exactly with the 96m. post the cutting recommences and this time the sides become ever steeper and the sky is a thin stripe when seen from track level.

At a depth of approximately 40ft. the cutting evens out and the railway now runs straight to pass under two bridges side by side, the first carrying the remains of the old roman road, the Fosse Way between Bath and Cirencester and the second a 2ft. square aqueduct. Still continuing straight a further occupation bridge passes overhead

The final cutting on the approach to Stoke Gifford with No. 5007 *Rougemont Castle* at the head of an eastbound express. In the background is the brakevan of a freight service and the signal can be seen to be lowered to route this latter train into the down loop.

National Railway Museum/G.H. Soole

marking the point at which the cutting deepens to over 60ft., so necessitating retained walls in places. Invisible from the railway itself but running parallel with the cutting is a sloping trench intended to carry water away to a number of drains. This continues until the line curves left to reveal the entrance to Alderton tunnel immediately ahead.

Of the two tunnels on the line Alderton is the shorter, and straight throughout its 506yd. length with interior brick walls 18in. thick made up of four separate rings. Staffordshire brindles, red brick and ashlar were used for the interior facings. The men working the permanent way gang over this stretch received a tunnel allowance of a few shillings each week which was payable whenever a tunnel was more than 440yds. long. Over the top of the tunnel runs the Grittleton to Luckington road; the GWR having originally purchased sufficient land north of the running lines to allow for a second tunnel if this was ever needed. Compared with Sodbury tunnel, the land above Alderton tunnel is almost level and raises the question why was a tunnel provided

A panoramic view of Stoke Gifford yard from the east end with the east signalbox on the left. The train is an 'up' local service from Bristol to Swindon stopping at all stations on the Badminton line and with a brand new 'Hall' No. 5940 *Whitbourne Hall* at its head.

National Railway Museum/G.H. Soole

when it would have been possible to continue with a cutting? The answer lies with local landownership with this particular landowner requiring that the railway be screened from view at this point.

Emerging into daylight from the tunnel, the cutting sides are steep but begin to slowly fall away in the course of which two more brick arched bridges pass overhead. Just over half a mile from the west end of the tunnel railway and surrounding land are once more combined, although the track is still climbing at a steady 1 in 300 and will continue to do so for a further mile. The area hereabouts is still principally farmland, although on the left a wood of both deciduous trees and conifers can be seen curving away for some distance in the direction of West Dunley Farm.

There is now a shallow embankment giving a view of open land to either side with on the up side of the line a minor stream which eventually passes into a culvert under the railway. Still on embankment the rails cross the Alderton to Little Drew road on a

On the main line at Stoke Gifford east, a 'Castle' hauled express passes a cutting full of a variety of wild flowers. In the background are bridges Nos. 302 & 303 whilst the course of the railway can be traced westwards for some distance until it disappears on the horizon.

National Railway Museum/G.H. Soole

skew bridge. Three more occupation bridges under then follow, the third near to the 99m. post, known as the welcome bridge by drivers of westbound trains as it is near the spot where the gradual rise changes to level line after which it is downhill all the way to the Severn tunnel. The summit of the line being some 387ft. above the ordnance datum. Another indicator of this change is the return to cutting and as the railway swings gently right it passes underneath the B4040, Acton Turville to Luckington Road at which point the old Saxon 'Centre Walk Avenue' also meets the public highway. As quickly as it began, the cutting subsides and is replaced by a very shallow embankment under which passes another farm track before entering the approaches to Badminton station.

Badminton is the nearest stopping place to the mid-point on the new line, its main station building coming after a small goods yard. Although the station took its name from the nearby country house the actual village of Badminton is some distance to the

The expanse of sidings at Stoke Gifford is well represented here, a number of which are laid with the wartime practice of concrete pot sleepers. The yards were extended at various times including 1918 when it was reported that two new goods loops were provided. As these connected at one end with the main lines the connections were inspected by the Board of Trade. The official report contained the unusual remark that the signalman in the east 'box had commented that additional signals were required and that the GWR had agreed to provide these.

C.G. Maggs

north of the railway and Acton Turville would have been a far more appropriate choice. However, in the best railway tradition the GWR dictated otherwise!

As the line passes under the road bridge at the west end of the station the cutting recommences, although it is just possible to catch a glimpse of the roof of the former Portcullis Hotel to the south, once a favourite with followers of the hunt. Today it is no more, although the hunt followers still gather to watch the men in their red and black coats as they set off.

Nowadays few passengers give a thought to the difficulties the contractors faced in this area with water penetrating the workings. But to the railway staff it was a continuing difficulty and clear instructions were issued detailing the course of action to be taken.

With the gradient now in favour of down trains this is the start of another very fast stretch of railway, the speed emphasised by the blur of the cutting sides as the line dips ever deeper into the ground with only two minor bridges and another overhead aquaduct to break the monotony. The steepness of the cutting sides varies between 4 in 1 and 1 in 1 depending on the solidity of the prevailing sub-strata. Onward then and curving gently right the cutting deepens even more becoming ever darker in the process until just past the 101m. post the sounds change and the railway enters the gloomy confines of Chipping Sodbury tunnel.

At 4444yds. in length, over 2mls. (although one early report quotes 4435yds.) this is one of the longest tunnels on the old Great Western and has always been regarded as a 'wet' tunnel. At the crown the curvature of the tunnel arch is 12ft. 6in., increasing to 15ft. 6in. at the walls before reducing to 9ft. 3in. The walls vary in thickness from 1ft. 6in. to 2ft. 3in. The railway company was very cautious over the running of trains through Sodbury tunnels and elaborate instructions were issued in the Sectional Appendix (see p. 159).

Above the tunnel it is mainly farmland, the six air-shafts which ventilated the bore standing gaunt against the Gloucestershire skyline. By each air-shaft there is a massive built-up mound, indicative of the material excavated when the shafts themselves were dug. Few roads pass over the top of the tunnel for the majority of its length, the exceptions being the Old Down Road, from Chipping Sodbury to Badminton, a private drive from Lyegrove House and what is now the main A46 between Bath and Nailsworth.

Near to the west end of the tunnel is the village of Old Sodbury and the railway passes directly beneath a number of premises. Emerging into daylight once more the railway is in a 50ft. deep cutting spanned by a three-arch brick bridge carrying a footpath over the line. Standing under the arch it is possible to hear the roar of water in the culvert beneath the rails which falls freely in the direction of Chipping Sodbury. Shortly afterwards a short section of level ground begins but still in a cutting. Here water troughs were laid with the supply obtained from an aqueduct crossing the railway at the east end and a natural brook under the railway some 400yds. further west. The aqueduct carries the embryo River Frome over the railway and was the subject of an unusual move by BR in 1986 when the banks of the river were strengthened which then in turn allowed the track level to be raised slightly and so reduce the frequency of flooding in the area, a change not possible at the time of construction as the level track had to be maintained for the water troughs. The end of the troughs is marked by a resumption of the 1 in 300 descent and a further three-arched brick bridge. Immediately following this is the start of Chipping Sodbury station yard the whole area excavated in a cutting of varying depth. The town of the same name lies to the north of the railway and with the stone quarry at right angles to the railway about a mile distant.

In recent times there has been much residential development to the north of the railway and some of this is visible above the top of the cutting sides. Much however is hidden from view as the line continues its path through a deep cutting which has gently sloping sides indicating an earth slip years before. Two further bridges cross the railway at this stage, both of which are brick structures, one marking the end of the station itself whilst the other a quarter mile further on, carries a minor road from Chipping Sodbury towards Kingrove Common.

The line now begins a gentle sweep to the left, still in cutting with Lillyput Road bridge crossing over it on the way from Codrington. Just south of the railway at this

Waiting to leave the yard for the east is a rther grimy 28xx No. 2812, the coal on the tender is a rather unusual looking mixture. The photograph is especially interesting as in the background there is a view of the private siding connection to Pugsley's yard on the site of the contractors former brickworks.

National Railway Museum/G.H. Soole

point was the famous Lillyput Quarry whilst a farm of the same name occupies a position on the opposite side of the line. Still curving left the cutting eases slightly before once more deepening with another small aqueduct overhead. The end of the cutting is marked by another brick bridge just past the 105m. post which precedes the start of the former government sidings at Wapley Common. These sidings were brought into use at intervals between 1.8.1941 and 1.7.1942 the access being controlled at first by a ground frame at either end.

The ground frame arrangement did not last long as on 1.7.1942 a new signalbox in the typical wartime GWR style was brought into use on the south of the main line. This controlled not only the eastern access and exit to and from the sidings, but was a block post in its own right working to Westerleigh East and Chipping Sodbury. The actual sidings included up and down loops as well as an up departure loop and two

In almost the same position No. 4941 *Llangedwyn Hall* awaits to set off, the fireman leaning out and evidently looking for the 'right away'. The water tower in the background is one of two at Stoke Gifford, each of 22,500 galls capacity and situated at either end of the yard. Contemporary reports suggest that consideration was given to a locomotive shed at Stoke Gifford in the early years of the century although with the close proximity of the various Bristol sheds the idea was eventually abandoned.

National Railway Museum/G.H. Soole

reception sidings. North east of the loops twelve futher sidings fanned out. The facilities officially remained in use until 1971 although the whole site has now been redeveloped as private housing.

Westerleigh East signalbox, less than ½m. west of the new Wapley Common 'box controlled not only the western connections from the sidings to the main line but also the eastern curve towards Westerleigh North and Yate. The east loop at Westerleigh had a chequered existence as apart from its on–off use prior to 1908 already previously recounted, the curve was taken out of use from 18.12.1916 until 18.2.1918, it however remained intact. It has not been possible to discern why this lack of use occurred. The loop was again taken out of use from 10.7.1927 and this time it is believed to have been

A beautifully clean No. 7825 *Lechlade Manor* in Stoke Gifford yard during late BR days.

Roger Sherlock

lifted whilst the signalboxes at Westerleigh East and North Junction were closed and demolished.

On the same date as Wapley Common 'box was opened the east curve at Westerleigh was re-opened and new signalboxes opened. The one at the north junction occupied the same site as the former 'box in the 'V' of the junction but Westerleigh East was now situated south of the main line on the same side as Wapley Common. The previous 'East 'box had been in the 'V' of the junction with the main line. (Full details and frame sizes etc for the Westerleigh 'boxes are given in Appendix E.)

At the end of the sidings a skew girder bridge crosses the railway and carries a private road to Sergeant's Farm which lies on the north side of the route. Immediately following is the east loop connection at Westerleigh and then one of the very few private level crossings on the whole route although affording access only to farmland. The ground is now falling away slightly and to compensate the railway rises on a wide embankment. To the right it is possible to see the west curve from Yate approaching the main line, the junction preceded by an under bridge carrying the Westerleigh to Yate road. The same road passes under the west curve with Bridge Farm hard by the railway.

Immediately afterwards the Midland main line can also be seen running north to south and with the Badminton route passing overhead by means of a three-arch viaduct. The course is now slightly to the right until the railway is running almost due west and still on embankment. In the course of this a brick-arched cattle creep leading to Dodmoor Farm passes underneath followed by a similar structure a few hundred yards later.

On the right now is Burnt Wood with a farm track to the left and parallel with the main line, this marks the course of an old mineral railway that once formed part of the colliery network in the area of Coalpit Heath. The railway is now approaching Coalpit Heath station. The first indication of this is as a single track mineral railway passes underneath the main line at right angles before disappearing north into the western edge of Burnt Wood. From the same mineral line a connection can be seen rising towards the main route on the right, this connecting into the colliery sidings now in view and also on the right.

Above the main line is a spindly girder bridge carrying a public footpath which crosses no less than six sets of rails before connecting in with Ram Hill Road to the south. Coalpit Heath station is similar to the other stations on the line, the mellow brickwork of the goods lock-up, signalbox and station buildings are a pleasant sight which blend in well with the woodland surrounding the station.

Hereabouts the land is dotted with old coal workings, one of which is only a few hundred yards south of the actual railway at a point where the coal seam rises to the land surface.

Passing over a three-arch bridge at the end of the station the railway crosses the Bristol to Coalpit Heath road. The original intention had been to erect an eight-arch viaduct, however, due to the number of old coal workings found in the vicinity there was concern for the stability for such a structure and a bridge and embankment were substituted. Continuing on its course of high embankment the railway reaches the next bridge over the main A423 road from Mangotsfield to Coalpit Heath and Yate. Mangotsfield of course was served by a station on the former Midland line and it is interesting to note that on a 1907 survey of the line the GWR failed to recognise even the public road as originating from this point and instead referred to the Bristol–Chipping Sodbury road! The delightfully named copse of Hotwater Brake is just south of the roadway.

Still on embankment which in places is nearly 70ft. feet high, the railway continues its path west over land formerly owned by Lady Emily Frances Smyth. It passes then over a footpath and a minor road known as Park Lane which leads to Frampton Cotterell village. Again greenery abounds at this point, although much of the remaining land is either farmland or in more recent years has been given over to development.

With the route now straight and still falling at 1 in 300, a drop of just over 17ft. 6in. in every mile, the embankment ceases and is replaced by the tallest of the viaducts on

Stanier Class '5' No. 44856 and 'Jubilee' No. 45573 *Newfoundland* double-head the north bound
'Devonian' inter-regional express (Paignton to Bradford) through Stoke Gifford in the late 1950s. In the
background lurks a 'Prairie' tank, although possibly of greater interest is the departmental sand van,
formerly an 'iron mink'.

G.F. Heiron

the railway, an eleven-arch brick structure known as Huckford viaduct under which
flows the River Frome having taken a northward circular path from its previous
crossing of the railway near Chipping Sodbury. From the viaduct's lofty stance of over
92ft. above ground level there is a grandstand view for miles around, including the
tops of trees on the valley floor as well as an old quarry and of course the meandering
course of the river itself.

Leaving the viaduct the railway immediately enters Winterbourne station, and the
final stopping place on the original route. Its basic up and down platform layout is a
repeat of that seen earlier and so we will not dwell on its facilities and instead continue
under another girder bridge after which is the station goods yard. With the end of the
goods yard also marking the end of Winterbourne village itself the railway crosses two
more roads and then surmounts the last viaduct under which runs Belgrave Road with
Bradley Brook alongside. The name Winterbourne is derivative of the term 'bourne'
or stream and as certain of the watercourses in the vicinity are known to dry up during

Stoke Gifford 111m. 56ch. (figures indicate capacity of sidings measured in four-wheeled vehicles).

One of the many 'Toad' brake vans allocated to Stoke Gifford although seen here far from its home depôt alongside the electrified lines in London.

H.M.R.S.

the summer months the name is singularly appropriate. The ground level here is particularly deceptive for although the viaduct is only five arches long the difference in height to the road and stream is 39ft. 3in. and 84ft. respectively, meaning that the slope at ground level is considerable. Part of this is explained by the fact that a number of old quarry workings are dotted around the area resulting in the road being built on refilled land.

Near this point the M4 was constructed in such a way as to allow the railway to cross the motorway on a steel and concrete bridge. The approaching junctions of Stoke Gifford causing the trains to pass over the road at slow speed and so probably fuelling the belief of the motorist that train travel is invariably slow. The old Gloucester road is next and this also marks the start of a brief level section of track. At this point also the embankment subsides to be replaced by a final cutting through the Pennant rock which is nearly 50ft. deep in places. Two occupation bridges then pass over the line, the second also affording clearance to a headshunt running alongside the up line. Immediately afterwards a clatter of pointwork heralds the approach to Stoke Gifford with the East signalbox on the south side of the down line.

Besides the up and down running lines there were originally six, but later as many

PRIVATE AND NOT FOR PUBLICATION.   Notice No. 364.

GREAT WESTERN RAILWAY.

Slipping Coaches at Stoke Gifford.

Commencing TUESDAY, MAY 22nd, 1923.

On week-days, commencing **Tuesday, May 22nd,** the 8.45 a.m. and 8.0 p.m. trains from Paddington to Fishguard Harbour will slip coaches for Bristol at Stoke Gifford at 10.48 a.m. and 10.2 p.m. respectively.

The coaches will be slipped when passing over the underbridge between $110\frac{3}{4}$ m.p. and 111 m.p. between Winterbourne and Stoke Gifford East Box, approximately half-a-mile from Stoke Gifford East Down Inner Home Signal, and must be brought to a stand just before reaching that signal.

The engine and coaches for Bristol to which the coaches slipped from the London train have to be attached must be standing in readiness on the Down Goods Loop Line at Stoke Gifford East. When the coaches slipped from the London-Fishguard train have come to a stand at the Down Inner Home Signal the engine and coaches standing on the Down Goods Loop Line must set back on to them, and the train when ready to leave must proceed to Bristol over the Down Main Line.

The standard instructions for slip carriage working shewn on pages 93-102 of the General Appendix to the Book of Rules and Regulations must be observed. Special attention is directed to Clauses 24 and 25 of those instructions.

The empty trains from Dr. Day's Bridge to Stoke Gifford, and the trains taking forward the coaches slipped from the London trains as shewn above, will run as under :—

	Arr. A.M.	Dep. A.M.	Arr. P.M.	Dep. P.M.
Dr. Day's Bridge	—	A 9†35	—	9†20 B
Stapleton Road	9/38		9/23	
Filton Junction	9/47		9/32	
Stoke Gifford West	9/49		9/34	
Stoke Gifford East	9†50	—	9†35	—

A Set No. 210.   B Brake-third.

	Arr. A.M.	Dep. A.M.	Arr. P.M.	Dep. P.M.
Stoke Gifford East	—	10 52	—	10 7
Stoke Gifford West	10/53		10/8	
Filton Junction Station	10/55		10/10	
Stapleton Road	S 10/59 W		10 14 SW	10 15 D
Temple Meads	11 3 C	11 15	10 20 E	—

C To form 11.15 a.m. Temple Meads to Weston-super-Mare.
D Precede 6.55 p.m. ex Swansea from Dr. Day's Bridge Junction.
E Empty train to go to Dr. Day's Bridge.

10.45 a.m. Clifton Down to Temple Meads.
To run to Old Station at Temple Meads.

10.5 p.m. Workmen's Train, Stoke Gifford to St. Philip's Marsh.
To run 5 minutes later throughout.

All concerned to note and arrange.

H. R. GRIFFITHS,
Divisional Superintendent.

Divisional Superintendent's Office,
Bristol, May 19th, 1923.

(300)   J. W. Arrowsmith Ltd., Printers, Quay Street, Bristol.

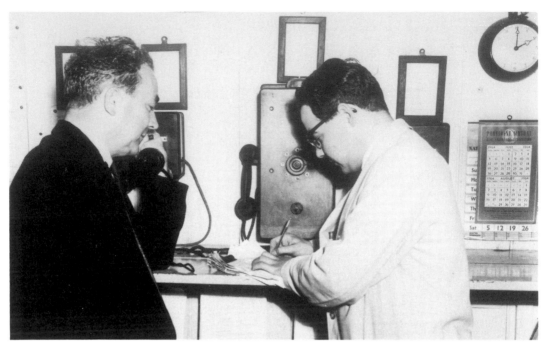

Staff at work in the goods office at Stoke Gifford in 1964.

British Railways

as ten, sidings on each side as well as loops and cripple sidings. On the north side another line can be seen curving away northeast to what was the former contractors brickworks but subsequently taken over by a private concern known as Pugsley's sidings. (An industrial estate was built on the site some years later.)

Invariably Stoke Gifford yard is full of vehicles of all shapes and descriptions, some already made up into trains whilst others await the attention of the shunter and pilot engine. The yard offices are on the south side of the railway with the west signalbox at the Newport end of the up side marshalling sidings. A terrace of GWR houses in their distinctive building style with alternate storeys of dark and light bricks occupy the side of a nearby road. Near to this point also the lines to Filton and Avonmouth diverge whilst the main route continues on its falling gradient towards Filton junction, the Severn tunnel and eventually Wales.

FIVE

CHANGING TIMES AND NEEDS

. . . the only way to be sure of catching a train is to miss the one before it.

G.K. Chesterton

In its original role as a main line and also as a rural railway the Badminton line had a life of just over sixty years. The first decade of British Railways' ownership brought little immediate change to what had been standard operating practices since 1903. There remained just a handful of stopping passenger services, although the majority of trains using the line (statistics record this as falling within the range of 0–99 trains daily) were the through services, both passenger and freight. Amongst the former category were, 'The Bristolian', 'The South Wales Pullman', 'The Pembroke Coast Express', 'The Capitals United' and 'The Red Dragon'. The last train listed was scheduled to call at Badminton in the down direction, a throwback to the earliest days when the GWR had promised to provide a first rate service to the station for the benefit of visitors to the house and area.

But apart from the regular passenger and goods services there were also a fair number of traction trials involving engines from Swindon. For many years these had involved steam traction but as would be expected with the passage of time so diesel types came to be used. The steam trials are already well recorded in the annals of locomotive history, although a number of the diesel tests may not be so well documented but they included the following types of modern traction between April 1961 and February 1963:

April	1961 –	Yorkshire Engine Co 0-8-0 diesel, *Taurus*
November	1961 –	'Warship' diesel, D821
December	1961 –	
January	1962 –	Brush 'Falcon' diesel, D0280
March	1962 –	'Hymek' diesel, D7011
April	1962 –	'Western' diesel, D1000
July	1962 –	'Lion' diesel
August	1962 –	
February	1963 –	Brush diesel, D1500

Apart from this particular use, the line was seen at railway headquarters as having two totally separate functions. Its principal use was its role as a main through route, with

The British Railways modernisation plan was announced publically in 1955 and this foretold the end of steam traction within a decade in practice this would take a little longer. Accordingly sights such as this were destined to become a feature of the past as No. 5094 *Tretower Castle* forges into a biting east wind with a Bristol–Paddington (via Badminton) express in January 1955.

G.F. Heiron

its secondary function being as a rural railway. It is convenient to describe the latter first which may also go some way to explaining the later changes.

Referring back to the individual stations it became abundantly clear that the railway market of the 1950s and '60s was very different when compared with the period from 1920 to 1939. Indeed a brief reference to the traffic statistics for the second period clearly shows how trade was rapidly falling away. The question may be asked then how and why did this occur?

To give an accurate answer to this question alone would occupy a considerable volume and it would also be singularly out of place in an individual railway history. However, it is worth pointing out that with the demands placed upon the railway network during a period of national emergency in the 1940s, it took time for services to be restored to anything like their pre-war level, although to a public tired of excuses for late running and dirty stock this was of little consolation. Into this equation must be brought the rapid development of the internal combustion engine in its various forms, 'buses, lorries and especially private motoring (which was enjoying an upsurge

Another superb snow scene this time with No. 70025 *Western Star* at the head of a South Wales to London service not far from Alderton tunnel.

G.F. Heiron

coinciding with the end of petrol rationing) and it becomes easy to see how the fare-paying passenger, and to an ever increasing extent the factory manager came to rely upon road haulage with its inherent flexibility compared with rail travel.

The question must be why didn't the railway counter such moves with new stock, better timings, renewed equipment etc? Unfortunately, the answer to this lies in the political arena and without wishing to enter the area of party politics it must be said that the now nationalised railway network was a sad victim of chronic underfunding from central government. As to whether the matter might have been any easier under private ownership must remain conjecture for rising wage costs and difficulty in attracting investment could well have resulted in a worse state than being under state control. To be absolutely blunt if it were not for the fact that the railways already existed no one in their right mind would have considered building such a system in the 1950s.

So what then was the answer? Certainly more investment and sooner rather than later as has occurred in practice. Possibly by remaining in private hands but with a degree of government funding and therefore control. The attraction being that the

1954 poster produced to advertise the 'Bristolian' service which ran via Badminton.

shareholders would still find an adequate return on their investment whilst the extra capital could be used in a more efficient way. Indeed as is now common knowledge, successive British governments have consistently spent far less of their gross national income on railway investment than almost any other European government. The failures of the 1950s would take more than a decade to put right and by that time a lot of ground had already been lost.

On the Badminton line, as indeed everywhere else on British Rail, it follows that means of achieving economies of working were sought. The first of these was the closure of the East loop at Westerleigh as from 4.1.1950 together with the now redundant North Junction signalbox. Whether BR had their doubts about the permanency of this move may be questioned, for the tracks remained *in situ* for a number of years and were not finally removed until 1967.

Table 8

THE RED DRAGON

RESTAURANT CAR SERVICE (¶)

LONDON, NEWPORT, CARDIFF, SWANSEA and CARMARTHEN

WEEK DAYS

	pm		am
London (Paddington) .. .. dep	5A55	Carmarthen .. .. dep	7A30
Swindon .. .. „	7 28	Ferryside .. .. „	7A42
Badminton .. .. „	7 58	Kidwelly .. .. „	7A50
Newport .. .. arr	8 47	Pembrey and Burry Port .. „	8A 0
Cardiff (General).. .. .. „	9 7	Llanelly.. .. .. „	8A10
Bridgend .. .. „	9 48	Loughor .. .. „	8A17
Port Talbot (General) .. „	10 8	Gowerton North .. .. „	8A22
Neath (General) .. .. .. „	10 21	Cockett.. .. .. „	8A30
Swansea (High Street) .. „	10 40	Swansea (High Street) .. „	8A45
Gowerton North .. .. „	10 58	Cardiff (General).. .. .. „	10A 0
Llanelly .. .. „	11 8	Newport .. .. „	10A20
Pembrey and Burry Port .. „	11 16	London (Paddington) .. .. arr	pm 1 0
Kidwelly .. .. „	11 28		
Ferryside .. .. „	11 36		
Carmarthen.. .. .. .. „	11 48		

A—Seats can be reserved in advance on payment of a fee of 2s. 0d. per seat (see page 23).

¶—Restaurant Car available between London (Paddington) and Cardiff (General), in each direction.

Perhaps the most prestigious service to serve the Badminton line was 'The Red Dragon' express, although this served Badminton station in the down direction only.

No. 6019 *King Henry V* working hard on the 1 in 300 climb through Chipping Sodbury station with the up 'Red Dragon' express.

G.F. Heiron

The stations remained open, albeit with ever dwindling local traffic, until Paddington decreeed that they would all, with one notable exception, close. The exception was Badminton, more of which shortly. Closure took effect from 3.4.1961, with goods facilities being withdrawn from Brinkworth and Coalpit Heath on the same day.

It is now appropriate to turn to the role the railway occupied as a through route for it was still the principal line into South Wales. As such the Beeching report of 1963 did not propose any major alterations to the route apart from the withdrawal of the remaining facilities from the intermediate stations. The Badminton line itself was seen as 'suitable for development'. But what was this development and how would it be realised? – at that time neither was at all clear.

To some extent the economies dictated by Beeching had already been started, as Little Somerford had been closed to freight from 10.6.1963 and there had been a similar reduction in facilities at Winterbourne on 7.8.1963. (The goods service to Malmesbury from Little Somerford ceased from 12.11.1962. It has not been possible to ascertain when goods facilities were withdrawn from Chipping Sodbury.)

At the regulation 20 m.p.h. speed, No. 5006 *Tregenna Castle* eases off the main line and into the down platform loop at Badminton with the down 'Red Dragon' in June 1953.

G.F. Heiron

Similar closures were, of course, occurring nationally, and so when goods services were withdrawn from Hullavington and Badminton on 4.10.1965 and 1.11.1966 respectively there was hardly a national outcry – the enthusiast was more concerned with the concurrent demise of steam and with it a number of secondary and branch lines. Despite the Badminton line itself remaining open, in line with national policy Wootton Bassett station was closed to passenger services from 4.1.1965 and to goods services on 4.10.1965.

One station was left of course, Badminton, but certainly not for the want of trying to close it! British Railways had originally scheduled Badminton for closure in 1961, but opposition from the Duke of Beaufort forestalled any such move. A further attempt to curtail the facilities was made a little later which again failed. Finally however Badminton was closed to passengers as from 3.6.1968. Even so the closure prompted Questions in the House!

Steam shunter at Stoke Gifford, No. 4131 crossing the main line an ATC ramp is just visible between the rails in the background.

Roger Sherlock

With all the stations now closed it would seem natural to expect that the next step would be the closure of the railway itself followed by the lifting of the track. But it must be remembered that the Badminton line was first and foremost a through route and accordngly this was far from being the end of the story and instead it is merely the start of a new chapter.

With the time now 1968, steam had already been abolished from the Western Region and preparations were in hand for the future introduction of the high speed diesel services of the 1970s and beyond. Consequently with the need for local traffic now removed time could be spent on upgrading the facilities for the future. This involved work in two areas, namely civil engineering and signalling. In connection with the first the whole route was closed for long periods at a time whilst new drainage, ballasting and track work was carried out. With the stations now non-existent as far as rail travel was concerned it was possible to effect minor changes to the track alignment

Introduced in 1925 to a design dating back to 1911, 73xx No. 7323 awaits departure from Stoke Gifford with a mineral train in October 1961.

Roger Sherlock

in the former station areas, although now the viability of the original 1897 construction was vindicated for little change was necessary. Indeed it is for this very reason that Brunel's main line along with the Badminton cut-off were chosen as the first lines to be equipped for HST working.

Referring now to signalling, progress on M.A.S. meant the previous mechanical arrangements were redundant (line occupancy had already been reduced with the closure of Brinkworth 'box in 1959) and with the advent of Bristol and Swindon panels the mechanical 'boxes were closed as follows:

Wootton Bassett East	24.3.1968
Wootton Bassett West	24.3.1968
Brinkworth	15.3.1959
Little Someford	18.6.1967

In its last years as the sole surviving stopping place on the new line, Badminton station was served by several main line trains. A 'Hymek' diesel awaiting departure with an evening Swansea to Paddington express. At this time the station was open from 7.0 a.m. to 9.0 p.m. daily and was in the charge of two porters who would alternate their turns of duty. Most of the station's passengers were London commuters.

G.F. Heiron

In many ways the diesel pullman units of the 1960s were the forerunners of the HST service and these were all at work on the Western Region towards the end of the decade. Here a six-car formation (excluding power cars), heads west from Chipping Sodbury tunnel with a down South Wales service. Notice the tunnel ventilation shaft visible on the skyline.

G.F. Heiron

Hullavington	24.3.1968
Badminton	10.5.1971
Chipping Sodbury	10.5.1971
Wapley Common	18.7.1965
Westerleigh East	10.5.1971
Westerleigh West	10.5.1971
Coalpit Heath	7.6.1964
Winterbourne	7.6.1970
Stoke Gifford East	21.2.1971
Stoke Gifford West	21.2.1971

The old and the new, a down pullman unit passing the wooden bracket signals at Westerleigh
Junction in 1968.

G.F. Heiron

Track maintenance in the 1960s, the latest equipment being used to replace the short sections of track with continuous welded rail. Notice the concrete post distant signal in the background (concrete post signals on the 'Western are themselves a fascinating story but unfortunately out of place in this volume), the view believed to have been taken near to Little Somerford.

British Railways

Almost the end at Stoke Gifford as a number of the yard staff pose in front of diesel shunter No. D3505 just prior to the yard's closure in 1971.

British Railways

Coalpit Heath in stark comparison to its days as a passenger station, shorn of its passing loops and
with the main building given over to private use. Several of the other station buildings and goods
sheds were also given over to industrial use following the withdrawal of railway faclities.

Courtney Haydon

By the early 1970s the line speed on the Badminton route was raised to 90 m.p.h.
throughout, with the junction connections at Wootton Bassett being suitable for
70 m.p.h. Running loops were also provided at Hullavington and Chipping Sodbury
whilst emergency crossovers were available at a number of locations. For the benefit of
the civil engineers a siding was retained at Hullavington.

This was but a foretaste of things to come for as resources became available the line
speed was raised to 125 m.p.h. over much of the route, whilst M.A.S. and further
corssovers allowed for far greater line occupancy as well as sections suitable for reverse
working. Alderton and Chipping Sodbury tunnels however are rated at 110 and 120
m.p.h. respectively, for the reason that the former is not ventilated.

Rationalisation elsewhere has meant that the former Midland main line south of
Yate through Mangotsfield has been closed and all traffic is now diverted via
Westerleigh and Filton. At Stoke Gifford there have been radical alterations, for with
the cessation of wagon load traffic in favour of bulk working, large marshalling yards
were a redundant asset. What would have been considered to have been an
impossibility sixty years ago occurred on 4.10.1971 when the yards closed. But from

Rebuilding the Badminton line in the early 1970s in preparation for the HST service. The first priority was improved drainage and so the old track had to be removed and the ballast dug out. A polythene membrane was then laid which would prevent soggy clay from 'pumping' upwards.

British Railways

After fresh ballast had been laid the pre-fabricated sections of track were unloaded and would later be welded together.

British Railways

Checking the alignment of the new track . . . muscle power alone on crow bars was sufficient to move the sections to provide the final alignment.

In certain areas where the ballast was in good condition all that was required was removal of the old track and the use of the trusty shovel to level the formation.

Sections of old bull-head track loaded and ready for removal.

All British Railways

the ashes of Stoke Gifford a phoenix has indeed arisen, and on the same site on 1.7.1972 BR opened a new Bristol Parkway station which was intended as a 'park and ride' facility.

To say that this has been a success is perhaps an understatement, and can be credited to a management determined to arrest the decline of the previous decade. Allied to this is the advent of the HST service bringing London to within little more than 75min. of Bristol; an incredible average speed in excess of 90 m.p.h. for over 100mls. In comparison the best time for steam traction was 30min. longer. Neither can this be considered the ultimate development, for in connection with the 'GWR150' celebrations a special HST working cut the London to Bristol time to a fraction over an hour running via Badminton. Unfortunately, nature still deems it necessary to take a part in the proceedings from time to time and despite all the railway's efforts, flooding is still a problem in certain areas.

Although today it is easy to be become complacent about speeds which eighty years ago could not even have been dreamed of, a recent run involving an up West of England HST may be of note. The service in question was booked to run non-stop from Taunton to Reading via Westbury, although signal failure at the latter location led to a rapid decision by Swindon control to change the route. The train was therefore

Where shunting engines once toiled twenty-four hours a day.... Bristol Parkway down platform, 1988.

K. J. Robertson

diverted via Bristol, Filton and Badminton, giving the opportunity for many miles of sustained high speeds and so reached Reading ahead of the normal booked time. Indeed it was necessary to stand for several minutes prior to the public departure time.

Such diversions have in some ways taken the place of the former local passenger services, somewhere Sir Weetman Pearson must surely be shaking hands with Mr Brunel.

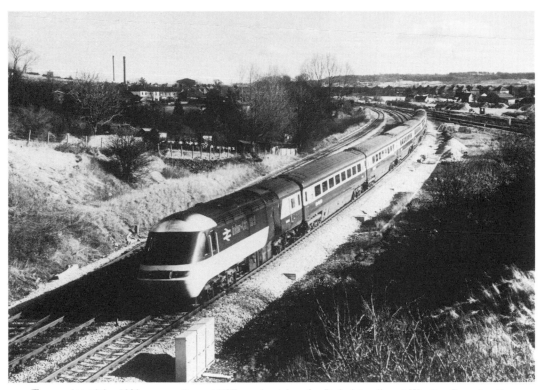

The service of the 1980s, an eastbound HST service takes the Badminton line at Wootton Bassett with a South Wales working.

G.F. Heiron

APPENDICES

APPENDIX A

GREAT WESTERN RAILWAY.

CONSTRUCTION OF A RAILWAY
BETWEEN
THE MAIN LINE NEAR WOOTTON BASSETT
AND
THE SEVERN TUNNEL RAILWAY NEAR PATCHWAY.
Total Length, including connecting Loops, about 33½ Miles.

TENDER.

To the DIRECTORS of the GREAT WESTERN RAILWAY COMPANY.

We, S. PEARSON & SON, LIMITED, of 10, Victoria Street, Westminster, S.W., having examined the Drawings and Specification of the above Works, do hereby agree to carry out such Works described and referred to in the Specification, and according to all the requirements, and upon the terms and conditions of the said Specification, and within the period of forty months, for the sum of Nine hundred and eighty-six thousand and eighty-four pounds, five shillings and twopence (£986,084 5s. 2d.).

And we have in the Schedule hereunto annexed set forth the prices of the different descriptions of work at which the aggregate of this Tender is computed, according to the approximate quantities supplied us, and which prices are to be the basis upon which the actual quantities of the work executed shall be measured up and paid for.

And we undertake to execute a Contract Deed to this effect, and to provide two good and satisfactory Sureties, who with us, jointly and severally, will enter into a Bond to the amount of £20,000, conditioned on the due fulfilment of the Contract.

Dated this 21ˢᵗ day of October, One Thousand Eight Hundred and Ninety-seven.

The Common Seal of S. Pearson & Son, Limited, was hereunto affixed in the presence of

W. D. Pearson
President.

S. Robinson
Secretary

Costs of stations and other major structures. (Note, tunnel No. 1 in the schedule was not constructed and was replaced by cutting.)

			@	£	s.	d.
		EARTHWORK.				
		Bill No. 3.				
		NOTE.—The Contractor's attention is called to the Earthwork diagram, Drawing No. 4.				
		The Company will hire to the Contractor rails for temporary roads. —See Specification.				
		The prices for excavation are to include all leads, forming into embankments, trimming slopes, forming side grips in cuttings and cross drains, and all contingencies as specified.				
1,039	cube yds.	Excavation in forming surface of existing embankment near commencement of Contract				
50,000	,,	Excavation in cutting No. 1, taken to embankment and tipped in lifts, not exceeding 14 ft. in height, as specified, &c.				
13,217	,,	Ditto ditto No. 2 ditto ditto ditto ...				
101,773	,,	Ditto ditto ,, 3 ditto ditto ditto ...				
144,829	,,	Ditto ditto ,, 4 ditto ditto ditto ...				
13,063	,,	Ditto ditto ,, 5 ditto ditto ditto ...				
39,000	,,	Ditto ditto ,, 6 ditto ditto ditto ...				
15,600	,,	Ditto ditto ,, 7 ditto ditto ditto ...				
95,927	,,	Ditto ditto ,, 8 forming into embankment, &c.				
98,150	,,	Ditto ditto ,, 9 ditto ditto ...				
286	,,	Ditto ditto ,, 10 ditto ditto ...				
100,000	,,	Ditto ditto ,, 11 ditto ditto ...				
110,000	,,	Ditto ditto ,, 12 ditto ditto ...				
193,441	,,	Ditto ditto ,, 13 between 20 m. 45 chs. and 21 m. 50 chs. ditto ditto...				
86,710	,,	Ditto ditto ,, 13 between 21 m. 50 chs. and 21 m. 70 chs. ditto ditto...				
10,000	,,	Ditto ditto ,, 13 between 21 m. 70 chs. and 22 m. 70 chs. ditto ditto...				
44,941	,,	Ditto ditto ,, 13 between 22 m. 70 chs. and 23 m. 58 chs. ditto ditto...				
42,950	,,	Ditto ditto ,, 14 ditto ditto ...				
40,575	,,	Ditto ditto ,, 15 ditto ditto ...				
80,000	,,	Ditto ditto ,, 16 ditto ditto ...				
7,824	,,	Ditto ditto ,, 17 ditto ditto ...				
1,757	,,	Ditto ditto ,, 18 ditto ditto ...				
1,151,082	,,	... ...	1/9	371,969	13	6
		Carried forward		**£** 371,969	13	6

			@	£	s.	d.
		Brought forward		371,969		6
16,000	cube yds.	Excavation in road approaches between 0 miles and 10 miles, to be conveyed to nearest embankments, &c.				
3,500	,,	Ditto between 10 miles and 18 miles, ditto				
1,500	,,	Ditto between 20 miles 45 chains and 24 miles, including branches 1, 2, 3, ditto				
19,000	,,	Ditto between 24 miles and termination of Contract, ditto				
40,000	,,	... ...	1/9	3,500	0	0
40,000	,,	Extra only in forming embanked road approaches, including all labour, trimming slopes, &c.	6d.	1,000	0	0
80,000	sq. yds.	Soiling and sowing slopes of cuttings as specified ...	4d.	1,333	6	8
119,000	,,	Ditto ditto ditto embankments ditto	4d.	1,983	6	8
10,000	cube yds.	Excavation for rubble drains in slopes of cuttings and embankments including timbering; average section 5 ft. by 3 ft. 6 in. wide	1/9	875	0	0
7,000	,,	Stone filling to ditto, obtained from the cuttings ...	3/-	1,050	0	0
2,000	,,	Burnt clay filling to ditto, including all fuel and labour as specified	5/-	500	0	0
5,000	,,	Burning clay and depositing same in making slips good, or as a toe to embankments as specified ...	5/-	1,250	0	0
1,000	,,	Excavation in seat of embankment, in trenching, or in special rubble drains as specified	1/9	87	10	0
1,000	,,	Stone filling to rubble drains obtained from cuttings...	3/-	150	0	0
1,000	,,	Burnt ballast to ditto, including all fuel and labour as specified	5/-	250	0	0
5,000	,,	Punning material in embankment to form toe as specified...	1/9	437	10	0
1,500	sup. yds.	18 in. pitching as specified	10/-	750	0	
1,500	,,	12 in. pitching as specified	7/6	562	10	0
		Carried to Summary	£	385,698	16	10

			@	£	s.	d.
		Brought forward.. ...		24,546	19	0
133	lin. ft.	Blue brick label course 1 ft. 6 in. by 6 in. by 6 in. ...	2 3	14	19	3
86	,,	Staffordshire blue brick coping, 18 in. by 6 in., set and jointed in cement	2 3	9	13	6
33	cube ft.	Pennant stone coping	4 -	6	12	0
73	cube yds.	Excavation in forming drain, as per drawing	3'-	10	19	0
1,320	lin. ft.	9 in. earthenware agricultural pipes laid end to end loose	1'-	66	0	0
100	cube yds.	Stone packing to ditto	2 6	12	10	0
100	,,	Lime concrete	15 -	75	0	0
		NOTE.—The value of any alteration in the thickness of the brickwork, ordered by the Engineer, will be added to or deducted from the Contract sum at the price per cube yard entered in this schedule for brickwork and excavation				
		Carried to Summary	£	24,742	12	9

Tunnel No. 3.

			@	£	s.	d.
319,836	cube yds.	Excavation for tunnel measured to back of brickwork, including all timbering, pumping and other contingencies as specified	8/-	127,934	8	0
26,136	,,	Masonry in mortar in side walls, including all cleaning and pointing	32/-			
		NOTE.—The Contractor is to insert a price for this item, but not to include the amount in the tunnel total				
26,136	,,	Brickwork in mortar in side walls, including all cleaning and pointing				
37,752	,,	Ditto in arch, including centering and all cleaning and pointing				
6,600	,,	Brickwork in mortar in invert, including all cleaning and pointing				
70,488	,,	... ...	31/-	109,256	8	0
10,220	,,	Excavation for ditto	8/-	4,088	0	0
133	lin. ft.	Blue brick label course, 1 ft. 6 in. by 6 in. by 6 in. ...	2/3	14	19	3
103	,,	Extra only to string course	1/-	5	3	0
288	cube ft.	Pennant stone coping	4/-	57	12	0
478	cube yds.	Masonry in mortar in facework of tunnel, including all cleaning and pointing	24/-	573	12	0
278	,,	Excavation in foundations and slopes for facework of tunnel	3/-	41	14	0
48	lin. ft.	3 in. earthenware pipes in weepholes	6d.	1	4	0
50	cube yds.	Lime concrete in foundations	15/-	37	10	0
		Carried forward	£	242,010	10	3

			@	£	s.	d.
		Brought forward		242,010	10	3
726	cube yds.	Excavation in forming drain	3/-	108	18	0
50	,,	Lime concrete to ditto	15/-	37	10	0
50	,,	Stone packing to ditto	2/6	6	5	0
3,068	lin. ft.	12 in. earthenware agricultural pipes laid end to end loose	1/6	980	2	0
5,140	cube yds.	Excavation in sinking shafts, including all timbering, pumping and other contingencies	27/-	6,939	0	0
690	,,	Brickwork in cement in permanent shafts, including pointing and all labours	36/-	1,242	0	0
80	lin. ft.	Blue brick curb in cement to underside of permanent shafts, including cutting and setting, and all labours	20/-	80	0	0
56	cube yds.	Masonry in mortar in shafts above ground, including cleaning and pointing	24/-	67	4	0
150	cube ft.	Pennant stone coping as specified	4/-	30	0	0
	No. 2	C.I. grating over tunnel shaft	25/-/-	50	0	0
	,, 150	Young trees planted round permanent shafts	5/-	37	10	0
100	lin. yds.	Post and wire fencing round ditto	2/6	12	10	0
2,770	cube yds.	Fill in temporary shafts with material punned hard and sound as specified	1/10½	259	13	9
5,000	sup. yds.	Levelling, trimming, soiling and sowing spoil heaps ...	4d.	83	6	8

NOTE.—The value of any alteration in the thickness of the brickwork, ordered by the Engineer, will be added to or deducted from the Contract sum at the price per cube yard entered in this schedule for brickwork and excavation.

			@	£	s.	d.
		Carried to Summary	£	251,944	9	8

			@	£	s.	d.

Bill No. 9.

STATION BUILDINGS, GOODS SHEDS, FOOTBRIDGES, &c.

(See specification for pricing these items.)

			@	£	s.	d.
11,243	cube ft.	**BRINKWORTH** Station Building	10½d.	491	17	7½
4,600	,,	Ditto Waiting Shed	9d.	172	10	0
17	squares	Platform coverings	16/-/-	272	0	0
No. 1		Cesspool, 5 ft. diameter by 8 ft. deep, etc., as specified	6/-/-	6	0	0
,, 1		Gun-metal pump, p.c. value £10, fixed complete ...	12/-/-	12	0	0
,, 1		Well lined with "Star" bricks in cement 9 in. thick, 3 ft. internal diameter, 30 ft. deep, covered with 3 in. stone and ring	50/-/-	50	0	0
,, 1		Inspection chamber, as specified		5	0	0
		Carried to Summary ... ... £		1,009	7	7½
11,243	cube ft.	**SOMERFORD** Station Buildings	10½d.	491	17	7½
4,600	,,	Ditto Waiting Shed	9d.	172	10	0
17	squares	Platform coverings	16/-/-	272	0	0
No. 1		Cesspool, as above...	6/-/-	6	0	0
,, 1		Pump as above, ...	12/-/-	12	0	0
,, 1		Well, as above	50/-/-	50	0	0
,, 1		Inspection chamber, as specified...		5	0	0
900	ft. run	Timber platforms as per drawings, including all struts, ties, stretchers, 3 in. planking, and bolts, etc., complete	12/-	540	0	0
		Carried to Summary ... ... £		1,549	7	7½

			@	£	s.	d.
11,243	cube ft.	**HULLAVINGTON** Station Building	10½d.	491	17	7½
4,600	,,	,, Waiting Shed	9d.	172	10	0
17	squares	Platform coverings	16/-/-	272	0	0
No. 1		Cesspool, as above		6	0	0
,, 1		Well, as above		50	0	0
,, 1		Pump, as above		12	0	0
,, 1		Inspection chamber, as specified		5	0	0
900	ft. run	Timber platforms, as per drawing	12/-	540	0	0
		Carried to Summary	£	1,549	7	7½
11,243	cube ft.	**BADMINTON** Station Building	10½d.	491	17	7½
7,475	,,	Ditto Waiting Shed	9d.	280	6	3
20	squares	Platform coverings	16/-/-	320	0	0
No. 1		Cesspool, as above		6	0	0
,, 1		Well, as above		50	0	0
,, 1		Pump, as above		12	0	0
,, 1		Inspection chamber, as specified		5	0	0
		Carried to Summary	£	1,165	3	10½
14,550	cube ft.	**CHIPPING SODBURY** Station Building	10½d.	636	11	3
7,475	,,	Ditto Waiting Shed	9d.	280	6	3
21½	squares	Platform coverings	16/-/-	344	0	0
No. 1		Cesspool, as above		6	0	0
,, 1		Well, as above		50	0	0
,, 1		Pump, as above		12	0	0
,, 1		Inspection chamber, as specified		5	0	0
		Carried to Summary	£	1,333	17	6

			@	£	s.	d.
11,243	cube ft.	**COAL PIT HEATH** Station Building	10½d	491	17	7½
4,600	,,	Ditto Waiting Shed	9d.	172	10	0
17	squares	Platform coverings	16/-/-	272	0	0
No. 1		Cesspool, as above		6	0	0
,, 1		Well, as above		50	0	0
,, 1		Pump, as above		12	0	0
,, 1		Inspection chamber, as specified		5	0	0
		Carried to Summary	£	1,009	7	7½
14,933	cube ft.	**WINTERBOURNE** Station Building	10½d	653	6	4½
4,602	,,	Ditto Waiting Shed	9d.	172	11	6
19¾	squares	Platform coverings	16/-/-	316	0	0
No. 1		Cesspool, as above		6	0	0
,, 1		Well, as above		50	0	0
,, 1		Pump, as above		12	0	0
,, 1		Inspection chamber, as specified		5	0	0
		Carried to Summary	£	1,214	17	10½
49,600	cube ft.	**CHIPPING SODBURY** Goods Shed	7½d	1,550	0	0
3,683	,,	Ditto ditto Office attached	10½d	161	2	7½
1¾	squares	Covering to Cart dock, including all iron and steel work, &c.	16 -/-	28	0	0
33	yds. sup.	Granite stone paving 5 in. by 4 in. thick, including concrete 6 in. thick	18/-	29	14	0
50	ft. run	Granite stone kerb 12 in. by 6 in., set in concrete ...	3 6	8	15	0
No. 2		Stone guards	20 -	2	0	0
		Carried to Summary	£	1,779	11	7½

			@	£	s.	d.
27,047	cube ft.	**WINTERBOURNE** Goods Shed	7½d.	845	4	4½
3,700	,,	Ditto ditto Office attached	10½d.	161	17	6
1¼	squares	Covering to Cart dock, including all iron and steel } work, &c. ... ... }	16/-/-	20	0	0
27	yds. sup.	Granite stone paving 5 in. by 4 in., including concrete } 12 in. thick ... ... }	18/-	24	6	0
44	ft. run	Granite stone kerb 12 in. by 6 in. set in concrete ...	3 6	7	14	0
No. 2		Stone guards	20/-	2	0	0
		Carried to Summary	£	1,061	1	10½
34,875	cube ft.	No. 5 Goods Lock-ups complete to level of rails ...	9d.	1,307	16	3
9,310	,,	No. 7 Weighbridge houses complete to ground level ...	7½d.	290	18	9
No. 7		Fixing Weighbridge machines, including excavation } and brickwork in pit ... ... }	40/-/-	280	0	0
,, 8		Four-line barrow roads, labour and all materials ...	36/-/-	288	0	0
,, 6		Two-line barrow roads, labour and all materials ...	18/-/-	108	0	0
		NOTE.—The totals for the above items are to be inclusive, and only altered in the event of any alteration in size or workmanship ordered by the Engineer.				
		Carried to Summary	£	2,274	15	0
		NOTE.—The following items apply to excavation, brickwork, &c., in foundations, &c., &c., and to Station footbridges, all of which are to be measured up and paid for at the prices entered in this Schedule.				
700	cube yds.	Excavation in foundations of Station Buildings, Goods } Sheds, Lock-ups, Weighbridge houses, cranes, &c. }	3/-	105	0	0
700	,,	Lime concrete in foundations	15/-	525	0	0
700	,,	Brickwork in mortar in foundations in piers and walls	32/-	1,120	0	0
50	,,	Brickwork in mortar in foundations in arches, in- } cluding centering ... ... }	34 6	86	5	0
		Carried forward	£	1,836	5	0

			@	£	s.	d.
		Brought forward		1,836	5	0
150	ft. lin.	Timber platform complete, including 3 in. deal planking, and all iron and steel work in " lock-up " platform walls	12/-	90	0	0
1,000	yds. sup.	Artificial stone coping, supplied by the Company, set in cement and bedded on 1¼ in. sand	4/6	225	0	0
2,100	lin. yds.	Fixing iron platform fence supplied by the Company...	3/-	315	0	0
	No. 14	Fixing iron exit gates in platform fence, supplied by the Company, including concrete foundations ...	30/-	21	0	0
400	lin. yds.	4 in. drain pipes, including digging, jointed in cement, including all bends, junctions, syphons and traps...	2/-	40	0	0
400	,,	6 in. ditto, ditto, ditto	3/-	60	0	0
2,000	,,	1½ in. lead supply pipe, 18 lbs. per yard, leading from well to pump, including digging and galvanized iron strainers tinned for lead and soldered. (All other lead pipes are included in the lump sum Tender for Station Buildings)	6/-	600	0	0
7,000	yds. sup.	Unloading, levelling, spreading, watering, rolling gravel 6 in. thick on platforms, supplied by the Company	8d.	233	6	8
3,000	ft. sup.	Damp course of two layers of slate in fine cement ...	4d.	50	0	0
700	cube yds.	Filling 2 ft. thick behind platform walls	1/6	52	10	0
	No. 3	Handling and erecting 5-ton cranes, supplied by the Company at Wootton Bassett or Filton. (The handling and erection of 30-cwt. cranes in Lock-ups and Goods Shed to be included in the price of the buildings)	30/-/-	90	0	0
300	ft. lin.	Oak cill 12 in. by 6 in. to " Lock-up " Platforms ...	4/-	60	0	0
	No. 120	Fixing lamp columns supplied by the Company, and painting three coats in approved oils... ...	20/-	120	0	0
		Carried to Summary	£	3,793	1	8

	@	£	s.	d.
## SUMMARY.				
Preliminaries and Contingencies ... ... Bill No. 1		5,000	0	0
Fencing ... ... ,, No. 2		19,616	13	4
Earthworks ... ... ,, No. 3		385,698	16	10
Ballasting and Metalling ... ... ,, No. 4		58,241	13	4
Permanent Way ... ... ••• ,, No. 5		9,535	0	0
Culverts and Drains ... ... ,, No. 6		20,713	4	1
Bridges, etc. ... ... ,, No. 7		115,065	5	0
Viaduct No. 1 ... ... ,, No. 8		9,702	13	0
Ditto No. 2 ... ... ,, ,,		15,854	2	0
Ditto No. 3 ... ... ,, ,,		23,944	0	6
Ditto No. 4 ... ... ••• ... ... ,, ,,		11,070	17	6
Tunnel No. 1 ... ... ,, ,,		13,433	19	3
Ditto No. 2 ... ... ,, ,,		24,742	12	9
Ditto No. 3 ... ... ,, ,,		251,944	9	8
Brinkworth Station Buildings, etc. ... . ,, No. 9		1,009	7	7½
Somerford ditto ditto ... ... ,, ,,		1,549	7	7½
Hullavington ditto ditto ... ... ,, ,,		1,549	7	7½
Badminton ditto ditto ... ... ,, ,,		1,165	3	10½
Chipping Sodbury ditto ditto ... ... ,, ,,		1,333	17	6
Coal Pit Heath ditto ditto ... ... ,, ,,		1,009	7	7½
Winterbourne ditto ditto ... ... ,, ,,		1,214	17	10½
Chipping Sodbury Goods Shed ... ... ,, ,,		1,779	11	7½
Winterbourne ditto ditto ... ... ,, ,,		1,061	1	10½
Lock-ups, Weighbridge houses, etc. ... ... ,, ,,		2,274	15	0
Foundations for above, etc., etc. ... ... ,, ,,		3,793	1	8
Footbridges... ... ... ,, ,,		3,780	18	0
TOTAL	£	986,084	5	2

Engineer's Office,
     Paddington, W.,
         August, 1897.

𝕿𝖍𝖎𝖘 𝕴𝖓𝖉𝖊𝖓𝖙𝖚𝖗𝖊 made the 21st day of October One thousand eight hundred and ninety seven **Between** S. Pearson & Son Limited whose Registered Office is at No. 10 Victoria Street in the City of Westminster and hereinafter called "the Contractors" of the one part and The Great Western Railway Company hereinafter called "the Company" of the other part **Whereby** the Contractors and the Company do mutually covenant and agree as follows, namely:—

First, **The** Contractors do hereby for themselves their successors and assigns covenant with the Company and their assigns that they the Contractors their successors and assigns shall and will perform observe fulfil obey and abide by the several articles clauses conditions and stipulations of the Tender and of the General Conditions and Specification of Works hereunto respectively annexed so far as the same respectively are to be performed observed fulfilled obeyed and abided by on the part of the Contractors.

Secondly **The** Company for themselves and their assigns covenant with the Contractors their executors and administrators that they the Company shall and will perform observe fulfil obey and abide by the several articles clauses conditions and stipulations of the said Tender and of the said General Conditions and Specification of Works so far as the same ○○

respectively are to be performed observed
fulfilled obeyed and abided by on
the part of the Company.
In witness whereof the Contractors and
the Company have caused their respective
Common Seals to be hereunto affixed the
day and year first before written.

The Common Seal of S.
Pearson & Son Limited
was hereunto affixed
in the presence of

The Common Seal of the
Great Western Railway
Company was hereunto
affixed in the presence of

W. D. Pearson

President

S. Robinson

Secretary

APPENDIX B

Statistics of traffic dealt with at station.

STATION	YEAR	Supervisory and Wages (all Grades) [No.]	Paybill Expenses [£]	TOTAL RECEIPTS [£]	Tickets issued [No.]	Season Tickets [No.]	Passengers (incl. Season tickets, etc.) [£]	Parcels [£]	Miscellaneous [£]	Total [£]	Coal and Coke 'Charged' Forwarded [Tons]	Other Minerals Forwarded [Tons]	General Merchandise Forwarded [Tons]	Coal and Coke 'Charged' Received [Tons]	Other Minerals Received [Tons]	General Merchandise Received [Tons]	Coal and Coke 'Not Charged' (Fwd & Rec) [Tons]	Total Goods Tonnage [Tons]	Total Receipts (excl. 'Not Charged' Coal and Coke) [£]	Livestock (Fwd & Rec) [Wagons]	Total Carted Tonnage (incl. in Total Goods Tonnage) [Tons]
Brinkworth to Pilning																					
Brinkworth (†)	1903	4	153	1,239	2,654	*	182	17	495	694	—	—	155	382	651	847	115	2,150	545	18	61
	1913	5	331	3,569	4,272	*	341	63	2,029	2,433	—	—	404	332	1,904	1,679	368	4,687	1,136	22	115
	1923	5	794	5,500	4,616	1	462	83	3,113	3,658	—	22	305	218	1,219	1,721	355	3,840	1,842	10	101
	1924	5	841	5,623	5,854	3	584	55	2,784	3,423	—	—	633	232	1,818	1,732	291	4,706	2,200	3	113
	1925	5	850	5,071	6,139	23	593	67	2,759	3,419	—	—	207	183	1,424	1,734	281	3,829	1,652	11	101
	1926	5	799	5,164	5,349	9	503	47	2,630	3,180	—	12	284	65	3,331	1,607	185	5,484	1,984	15	99
	1927	5	848	5,242	3,389	10	347	45	2,802	3,194	31	—	552	213	912	1,821	167	3,696	2,048	11	102
	1928	5	813	4,919	2,725	7	292	62	2,728	3,082	—	6	532	60	1,431	1,318	129	3,476	1,837	13	67
	1929	5	805	4,883	2,365	10	270	62	2,744	3,076	—	—	410	49	1,982	1,274	135	3,850	1,807	8	66
	1930	5	784	3,859	2,091	10	218	52	2,434	2,704	—	—	291	57	289	971	151	1,759	1,155	14	56
	1931	5	801	2,240	1,989	7	227	36	1,181	1,444	—	—	151	25	26	842	169	1,213	796	22	53
	1932	4	566	1,938	1,943	12	212	38	1,059	1,309	—	—	101	39	63	704	149	1,019	629	12	101
	1933	4	560	1,808	2,436	9	243	39	663	945	—	—	415	35	—	515	129	1,157	863	12	234
Little Somerford	1903	6	245	1,675	2,021	*	245	23	235	503	—	—	71	340	1,326	279	—	2,334	1,172	136	57
	1913	6	373	3,862	4,662	*	778	138	1,104	2,020	—	17	612	242	1,968	3,146	479	6,464	1,842	130	130
	1923	7	1,003	7,574	4,764	4	661	134	2,543	3,338	—	—	1,104	485	1,287	3,722	839	7,437	4,236	98	175
	1924	7	1,087	6,396	4,120	3	730	121	1,961	2,812	—	—	478	594	2,296	3,551	960	7,879	3,584	137	157
	1925	7	1,143	5,653	4,228	—	752	110	1,790	2,652	—	—	378	559	2,481	3,003	928	7,344	3,001	162	191
	1926	7	1,038	5,309	3,515	—	603	76	1,734	2,413	—	19	220	374	2,151	2,978	711	6,453	2,896	205	190
	1927	7	1,063	6,105	2,947	5	525	75	2,058	2,658	13	20	479	590	1,345	2,895	909	6,251	3,447	190	226
	1928	6	1,017	5,653	2,361	—	414	64	2,121	2,599	—	37	354	613	1,736	2,700	633	6,073	3,054	194	103
	1929	6	1,000	5,045	2,335	—	440	69	1,885	2,394	—	14	213	611	339	2,509	809	4,555	2,651	239	84
	1930	6	1,041	4,729	2,071	—	350	65	2,181	2,596	—	14	208	399	147	2,677	855	4,300	2,133	94	85
	1931	6	983	4,715	1,937	—	306	73	1,677	2,056	—	12	230	289	19	3,878	977	5,405	2,659	110	74
	1932	6	976	3,373	1,753	—	269	55	445	769	—	28	354	311	42	4,002	956	5,693	2,604	80	335
	1933	7	1,027	3,479	2,853	1	374	52	62	488	—	34	384	286	52	4,374	1,084	6,214	2,991	82	563
Hullavington	1903	6	191	1,471	2,316	*	300	47	69	416	—	—	671	506	1,115	721	1,283	4,296	1,055	19	105
	1913	7	348	4,234	3,902	*	584	181	1,511	2,276	—	—	1,250	1,368	3,627	1,897	1,185	9,327	1,958	63	257
	1923	7	1,316	7,227	3,510	4	676	307	3,529	4,522	13	—	729	1,583	674	1,838	1,211	6,048	2,705	42	199
	1924	7	1,194	7,658	3,431	4	790	277	3,529	4,596	10	6	807	1,454	524	2,180	1,732	6,713	3,062	43	223
	1925	7	1,208	7,626	3,133	—	662	279	3,446	4,387	—	34	1,484	1,230	885	1,924	2,150	7,707	3,239	33	269
	1926	7	1,107	6,661	2,927	4	644	232	3,221	4,097	10	216	868	471	982	1,656	2,041	6,244	2,564	38	235
	1927	7	1,214	6,593	2,483	13	544	247	2,850	3,641	5	249	861	1,086	2,284	1,651	3,019	9,155	2,952	31	236
	1928	7	1,126	6,196	2,602	8	515	197	2,923	3,635	—	18	810	1,423	945	1,347	2,205	6,748	2,561	46	118
	1929	7	1,141	6,262	2,459	6	481	188	3,222	3,891	—	117	836	1,129	1,149	1,294	2,406	6,931	2,371	53	127
	1930	7	1,173	5,377	2,475	3	456	198	3,064	3,718	8	61	295	989	429	1,418	2,450	5,650	1,659	34	127
	1931	6	1,021	4,696	1,962	2	367	165	2,629	3,161	—	—	246	862	628	1,430	2,629	5,795	1,535	27	102
	1932	5	995	3,362	1,827	1	350	139	1,815	2,304	10	—	147	832	164	742	2,567	4,462	1,058	25	174
	1933	5	853	1,819	1,692	1	332	121	308	761	—	—	410	999	108	517	2,509	4,543	1,058	32	249
Badminton	1903	9	289	3,088	8,332	*	1,011	148	357	1,516	—	7	692	700	1,440	3,107	2,323	8,269	1,572	48	383
	1913	7	513	7,494	14,656	*	2,298	435	1,271	4,004	5	15	2,326	4,669	3,168	6,005	1,929	18,117	3,490	75	967
	1923	10	1,610	11,294	11,358	70	3,799	407	3,088	7,294	12	—	2,215	3,453	363	3,684	2,683	12,410	4,000	49	570
	1924	10	1,574	10,929	11,219	53	3,681	426	3,174	7,281	—	37	1,322	3,196	273	3,859	3,155	11,842	3,648	84	641
	1925	10	1,583	10,950	11,354	46	3,206	387	3,710	7,303	—	28	1,778	3,116	360	3,291	2,851	11,474	3,647	55	597
	1926	14	1,549	10,698	9,952	28	2,676	348	4,007	7,031	12	16	1,561	1,767	765	3,237	2,067	9,425	3,667	76	600
	1927	14	1,843	12,533	9,865	35	2,754	354	5,327	8,435	12	43	1,436	2,401	653	3,528	3,743	11,816	4,098	73	603
	1928	14	2,090	13,160	9,663	13	2,746	402	6,210	9,358	—	36	1,389	3,576	398	3,153	2,278	10,830	3,802	72	511
	1929	14	2,151	13,209	8,850	13	2,548	420	6,692	9,660	—	—	841	3,490	386	3,119	2,678	10,487	3,549	89	454
	1930	13	1,952	11,563	8,436	15	2,405	332	5,645	8,382	—	50	631	3,164	440	2,319	2,514	9,430	3,181	53	426
	1931	11	1,936	13,591	7,174	17	2,102	308	4,273	6,683	—	9	917	2,353	265	6,811	3,334	13,689	6,908	54	474
	1932	10	1,556	7,191	6,406	13	1,827	282	2,540	4,649	—	62	502	2,310	129	2,562	2,596	8,161	2,542	54	990
	1933	9	1,387	5,032	5,684	7	1,792	330	895	3,017	—	23	388	2,097	153	2,045	2,111	6,817	2,015	40	1,281
Chipping Sodbury	1903	10	368	2,742	7,659	*	682	56	91	829	—	5,584	1,080	117	1,417	562	598	9,308	1,913	7	255
	1913	7	663	4,813	15,557	49	1,353	152	635	2,140	24	12,801	490	1,104	1,571	1,936	595	17,997	2,673	67	636
	1923	12	1,961	17,543	6,079	49	1,093	215	333	1,641	24	33,945	464	1,482	646	2,640	3,304	42,505	15,902	77	543
	1924	12	1,972	16,687	6,888	65	1,393	196	386	1,975	24	39,481	321	1,958	917	2,541	3,329	48,581	14,712	85	511
	1925	11	1,965	17,252	7,004	56	1,168	201	261	1,630	—	53,410	461	2,154	791	2,063	3,848	62,727	15,622	75	521
	1926	11	1,832	26,786	5,205	28	1,030	198	270	1,498	10	76,465	417	1,377	583	2,451	2,308	83,611	25,288	61	572
	1927	11	1,932	28,473	5,623	78	991	181	195	1,367	15	69,225	827	1,449	562	2,956	3,379	78,419	27,106	56	649
	1928	12	1,918	32,456	5,649	101	1,009	214	194	1,417	—	71,011	1,950	1,655	909	3,012	2,772	81,309	31,039	102	570
	1929	12	1,998	29,492	3,547	77	793	239	197	1,229	8	63,363	955	994	833	2,691	3,982	72,824	26,263	84	598
	1930	12	1,922	32,840	3,547	57	609	253	143	1,005	—	76,712	486	697	261	3,199	3,870	85,216	31,835	100	632
	1931	12	1,866	35,296	3,095	41	505	243	110	858	31	87,680	551	496	392	2,450	4,214	95,814	34,438	54	614
	1932	12	1,850	32,282	2,751	51	559	194	114	867	—	77,525	611	269	136	2,578	3,345	84,464	31,415	49	534
	1933	13	1,904	31,003	3,303	94	575	181	85	884	—	79,279	802	265	382	2,878	2,830	86,426	30,159	39	681

STATION	YEAR	STAFF			PASSENGER TRAIN TRAFFIC									GOODS TRAIN TRAFFIC										
					Tickets issued	Season Tickets	Receipts				Forwarded			Received										
		Supervisory and Wages (all Grades)	Payroll Expenses	TOTAL RECEIPTS			Passengers (including Season tickets, etc.)	Parcels	Miscellaneous	Total	Coal and Coke 'Charged'	Other Minerals	General Merchandise	Coal and Coke 'Charged'	Other Minerals	General Merchandise	Coal and Coke 'Not Charged' (Forwarded and Received)	Total Goods Tonnage	Total Receipts (excluding 'Not Charged' Coal and Coke)	Livestock (Forwarded and Received)	Total Carted Tonnage (included in Total Goods Tonnage)
		No.	£	£	No.	No.	£	£	£	£	Tons.	Tons.	Tons.	Tons.	Tons.	Tons.	Tons.	Tons.	£	Wagons	Tons.
Coalpit Heath	1903	5	150	453	7,821	*	429	20	4	453				Opened for Goods Traffic c. 1904							
	1913	6	435	3,893	13,389	*	823	57	31	911	34,327	—	254	59	366	1,042	48	36,096	2,982	—	128
	1923	6	1,012	5,114	4,911	74	554	64	45	663	31,769	—	40	132	193	972	59	33,165	4,451	—	150
	1924	6	991	3,788	5,345	40	579	74	62	715	22,511	—	42	22	78	1,096	190	23,939	3,073	—	158
	1925	6	1,026	4,916	5,463	69	597	71	96	764	31,773	—	118	4	139	833	266	33,133	4,152	—	163
	1926	6	932	2,478	4,767	200	521	98	45	664	11,708	—	51	25	205	636	303	12,928	1,814	—	137
	1927	6	992	3,088	4,412	252	554	156	40	750	14,876	74	42	10	124	818	376	16,320	2,338	1	157
	1928	6	910	4,383	3,893	213	454	141	94	689	26,110	13	67	—	109	1,026	345	27,670	3,694	2	87
	1929	6	951	5,773	3,090	154	387	152	121	660	38,094	—	39	—	173	706	652	39,664	5,113	3	81
	1930	6	956	5,839	2,067	81	258	170	109	537	44,337	—	23	—	98	657	306	45,421	5,302	6	88
	1931	6	933	4,870	2,147	49	257	176	130	563	32,539	6	43	4	108	684	134	33,518	4,307	5	101
	1932	6	925	5,209	2,150	81	276	183	93	552	29,369	—	37	—	72	723	741	30,942	4,657	·1	89
	1933	6	907	6,384	2,425	75	346	159	13	518	29,962	22	45	—	98	636	58	30,821	5,366	1	87
Winterbourne (†)	1903	8	206	1,093	13,476	*	704	30	18	752	—	1,653	106	153	210	134	1,373	3,629	341	11	77
	1913	5	351	2,689	23,187	*	1,252	69	18	1,339	9	2,051	181	2,039	1,038	500	1,401	7,219	1,350	49	165
	1923	6	833	2,843	8,944	59	694	125	241	1,060	—	1,607	88	2,446	51	650	867	5,709	1,783	36	157
	1924	6	798	3,548	7,844	44	713	144	185	1,042	—	4,533	78	2,456	178	880	1,100	9,225	2,496	16	179
	1925	5	836	3,682	8,208	37	730	115	140	985	—	3,661	132	2,495	190	767	1,086	8,331	2,697	35	189
	1926	5	806	3,429	6,669	28	515	85	54	654	—	4,385	63	1,604	52	754	1,182	8,040	2,775	18	174
	1927	5	845	2,993	5,888	39	452	84	145	681	7	2,311	89	1,858	74	521	1,501	6,361	2,312	34	207
	1928	5	838	2,407	4,935	30	446	84	73	603	9	1,759	157	2,021	48	332	965	5,291	1,804	52	92
	1929	5	803	2,211	4,159	59	395	92	89	576	5	2,026	53	1,947	92	330	1,060	5,513	1,635	25	140
	1930	4	738	1,542	3,646	30	341	103	61	505	—	510	39	1,774	75	232	1,128	3,758	1,037	20	92
	1931	3	615	1,302	3,512	13	333	84	24	441	—	292	16	1,451	97	220	1,189	3,265	861	29	86
	1932	3	411	1,048	2,976	32	309	89	25	423	—	98	16	1,277	34	170	1,059	2,654	625	13	78
	1933	3	378	1,064	4,243	24	370	71	32	472	—	117	19	1,009	18	160	1,428	2,811	591	9	84
Wootton Bassett	1903	22	1,463	16,378	55,263	*	2,323	488	5,553	8,364	8	107	4,172	2,868	4,433	7,498	2,726	21,812	8,014	182	2,263
	1913	19	1,497	16,187	47,131	*	2,274	443	6,913	9,630	16	67	3,327	2,559	4,905	5,528	2,359	18,451	6,557	155	1,935
	1923	22	3,808	27,523	38,782	599	3,127	578	13,149	16,854	—	133	3,729	2,769	4,595	4,070	3,428	18,725	10,669	272	1,551
	1924	22	3,699	24,868	41,434	690	3,272	578	11,317	15,167	—	151	2,672	1,968	4,057	4,594	3,749	17,191	9,701	233	2,080
	1925	22	3,766	24,815	44,124	825	3,454	598	11,268	15,320	32	102	2,855	2,158	3,367	4,477	4,081	17,072	9,495	255	1,559
	1926	22	3,601	24,064	42,753	752	3,194	575	11,334	15,103	38	71	1,940	2,363	3,707	4,771	2,964	15,854	8,961	240	1,555
	1927	22	3,650	27,835	46,693	711	3,283	548	11,622	15,453	—	168	2,601	1,629	10,942	4,963	4,855	25,258	12,382	184	1,500
	1928	22	3,620	26,748	45,157	781	3,075	552	14,282	17,909	—	103	2,140	747	4,760	4,389	5,487	17,596	8,839	277	1,273
	1929	22	3,504	26,191	42,580	792	3,044	532	15,036	18,612	22	94	1,451	757	1,965	4,272	5,541	14,102	7,579	259	1,166
	1930	22	3,514	24,308	42,000	792	2,865	365	13,720	16,950	29	268	1,502	818	3,206	3,963	7,089	16,875	7,458	246	1,099
	1931	21	3,417	27,502	40,617	717	2,518	356	15,648	18,522	34	174	2,526	556	1,975	4,662	8,530	18,457	8,980	170	1,228
	1932	21	3,226	33,587	37,415	665	2,420	274	24,234	26,928	—	176	933	441	1,380	5,295	6,573	14,798	6,659	135	1,372
	1933	20	3,223	41,828	32,112	611	2,177	202	32,731	35,200	—	415	1,387	234	2,618	4,734	6,903	16,291	6,628	140	2,262

Additional references to traffic dealt with at stations. (Coal tonnage in brackets and included in main total.)

Wootton Basset

	No of Passengers	Passenger receipts	Parcels receipts	Goods tonnage
Jan – Nov 1938	39,242	£2,453	£19,668	11,926 (5,120)
Jan – Nov 1946	58,062	6,545	24,799	14,574 (6,656)

Brinkworth

	No of Passengers	Passenger receipts	Parcels receipts	Goods tonnage
Jan – Nov 1938	2,021	191	146	570 (87)
Jan – Nov 1946	1,569	232	36	–

Little Somerford

	No of Passengers	Passenger receipts	Parcels receipts	Goods tonnage
Jan – Nov 1938	3,837	360	69	3,987 (3,066)
Jan – Nov 1946	4,020	622	175	2,765 (1,576)

Hullavington

	No of Passengers	Passenger receipts	Parcels receipts	Goods tonnage
Jan – Nov 1938	5,930	1,500	202	12,725 (6,153)
Jan – Nov 1946	3,129	1,025	244	8,571 (6,745)

Badminton

	No of Passengers	Passenger receipts	Parcels receipts	Goods tonnage
Jan – Nov 1938	5,224	1,959	1,397	5,698 (3,824)
Jan – Nov 1946	7,077	4,821	1,156	9,787 (3,176)

Chipping Sodbury

	No of Passengers	Passenger receipts	Parcels receipts	Goods tonnage
Jan – Nov 1938	2,075	372	115	25,647 (3,804)
Jan – Nov 1946	1,505	676	409	2,0443 (5,834)

Coalpit Heath

	No of Passengers	Passenger receipts	Parcels receipts	Goods tonnage
Jan – Nov 1938	1,747	198	53	22,175 (21,695)
Jan – Nov 1946	907	141	81	22,637 (27,504)

Winterbourne

	No of Passengers	Passenger receipts	Parcels receipts	Goods tonnage
Jan – Nov 1938	3,651	298	61	3,694 (3,434)
Jan – Nov 1946	2,390	335	105	3,860 (2,855)

APPENDIX C

Staff as at May 1918 – (Note: although compiled from official sources it is likely that a number of female staff who had replaced men during from 1914 onwards were still employed. With one possible exception they are not shown on the permanent staff lists. It should be remembered also that this was prior to the general introduction of the 8-hour working day.)

WOOTTON BASSETT

Station master	M. Campfield
Signalmen	John Bennett
	Edwin Thorne
	Henry Ogborne
	Alfred Bond
	George Mitchell
	Henry Fellender
	Alf Goddard
	Herbert Potter
	William Garvey
First class district reliefman	Frederick Cook
Checker	Percival Bond
District lampman	William Hodges
Parcel porters	Robert Collins
	Frederick Willoughby
Porter/Shunters	Alfred Stinchcomb
	Percy Boyce
	Sidney Joyce
Goods porters	Frederick Ogborn
	Hubert Moore

BRINKWORTH

Station master	Edward Axe
Signalmen	William Dodds
	Arthur Nicholls
Porters	Albert Freeborn
	Frank Knibbs

LITTLE SOMERFORD

Station master	Henry Jefferies
Signalmen	Edward Hasell
	George Thomas
	George Osborne
Porters	Frederick Clarke
	Herbert Wakely
	Edward Dunning

HULLAVINGTON

Station master	Albert Jefferies
Signalmen	Victor Allen
	Henry Old
	Ernest Bishop
Porters	Walter Mason
	George Lewis
	Edgar Small

BADMINTON

Station master	M. Randall
Signalmen	John Newman
	Albert Toogood
Goods porters	William Newman
	Merson Newman
Porters	Ernest Clark
	William Liner

CHIPPING SODBURY

Station master	M. Carter
Signalmen	George Bacon
	Arthur Back
	Reginald Lacey
	Thomas Strong
	Aaron Jefford
	William Smith
	Chas Hicks

CHIPPING SODBURY

Checker	George Osborne
District lampman	William Bennett
Porters	Henry Mustey
	Reginald Dyke

COALPIT HEATH

Station master	Eliah Barrington
Signalmen	John Shergoed
	William Scoble
	Henry Packer
Porters	Arthur Westcott
	Leonard Eveleigh
District lampman	William Leonard

WINTERBOURNE

Station master	William Glasson
Signalmen	William Carter
	James Smith
Porter	(Miss ?) C. Sims
Signal/Porter	Arthur Westcott

STOKE GIFFORD YARD

Chief Yard inspector	Silas Pitt
Yard inspectors	James Bobbett
	Frederick Edmunds
	George Hellier
	William Richards
	William Stone

Approximately	24 Goods guards
	6 Signalmen
	22 Head shunters
	9 Under shunters
	2 Lad porters
	2 Lampmen, first class

APPENDIX D

List of permanent way gangs and lengths covered – *c.*1935. (Taken from official records.)

Each permanent way gang consisted of an average of 6–8 lengthmen under the control of a sub-ganger and ganger. The length of track under the care of each gang depended upon the likely level of maintenance required. The ganger would walk the length daily to check for failures and was responsible for track and fencing maintenance in his area. As a general rule the summer months were spent on keeping the vegetation in check whilst the winter months were occupied with trackwork. For major repairs assistance would be sought from neighbouring or the district-based relaying gang. Along each length huts for the use of the men were placed at intervals and besides being used as shelters they contained tools and other equipment. Gangs came under the control of a Permanent Way Inspector, one of whom was based at Chipping Sodbury.

BRISTOL ENGINEERS DISTRICT

Gang No.	Mileage	
13	Wootton Bassett main line and Junction to South Wales.	
61	83m. 30ch. – 85m. 70ch.	(Wootton Bassett to east of Brinkworth.)
	6285m. 70ch. – 88m. 30ch.	(East of Brinkworth to just over 1m. east of Little Somerford.)
63	88m. 30ch. – 90m. 70ch.	including Malmesbury Branch. (Just over one mile east of Little Somerford to just west of Little Somerford viaduct.)
64	90m. 70ch. – 93m. 30ch.	(Just west of Little Somerford viaduct to Bridge No. 251, approximately 1m. east of Hullavington.)
65	93m. 30ch. – 95m. 70ch.	(Bridge No. 251 to Pig lane, bridge No. 259.)
66	95m. 70ch. – 98m. 30ch.	(Pig Lane Bridge to approximately m. west of Alderton tunnel and including the tunnel itself.)
67	98m. 30ch. – 100m. 70ch.	(m. west of Alderton tunnel to just over m. west of Badminton station.)
68	100m. 70ch. – 102m. 40ch.	(Just over m. west of Badminton to mid-point in Chipping Sodbury tunnel)
69	102m. 40ch. – 104m. 20ch.	(mid-point in Chipping Sodbury tunnel to immediately east of Chipping Sodbury station.)

70	104m. 20ch. – 106m. 60ch.	and to 106m. 78ch. in Yate loop. (East of Chipping Sodbury station approximate mid-point between Westerleigh East and West signalboxes.)
71	106m. 60ch. – 108m. 65ch.	and Yate branch connections. (mid-point between Westerleigh East and West signalboxes to ½m. west of Coalpit Heath station.)
72	108m. 65ch. – 111m. 25ch.	(1m. west of Coalpit Heath station to Stoke Gifford East signalbox and including connections at the east end of the yard.)
73	111m. 25ch. – 112m.	and including connections west of Stoke Gifford.

APPENDIX E

Signalbox details, Westerleigh East, West and North 'boxes:

Westerleigh East	Opened 1.5.1903. Brick construction. 21ft. x 12ft. x 8ft. to operating floor. 23 lever frame and fitted with block switch. 'Box closed and demolished 10.7.1927. 2nd 'box, opened 1.7.1942. Brick construction. 33ft. 6in. x 13ft. x 10ft. 6in. to operating floor. 44-lever frame at 4in. centres with vertical tappet 3-bar locking. Fitted with block switch.
Westerleigh West	Opened 1.5.1903. Same design as Little Somerford and Brinkworth. 21ft. x 12ft. x 8ft. to floor. 23 levers at 5in. centres and fitted with stud locking. Block switch provided.
Westerleigh North	Opened 1.5.1903. Timber construction. 21ft. x 12ft. x 8ft. to floor. Fitted with 23 lever frame and block switch. 'Box closed and demolished 10.7.1927. 2nd 'box, opened 16.8.1942. Timber construction. 20ft. 2in. x 12ft. 2in. x 8ft. to floor. 23 lever frame at 4in. centres with 5-bar vertical tappet locking. Block switch provided.

APPENDIX F

Reports on condition of Alderton tunnel, 506yds., 1932–1953. (Taken from official reports.)

27.11.1932 Good.
22.10.1933 Generally good, but pointing required on soffitt at both ends, and the west face requires pointing.
28.10.1934 No change from 1933, and repairs recommended then still awaited.
22.11.1936 Good condition, water percolates through soffitt near Badminton end but not serious.
13.11.1938 Brickwork in good condition, no repairs required.
 3.3.1940 Good, but two new down pipes needed.
31.8.1941 Good.
29.4.1945 Brickwork fine with the exception of two patches at each end approximately 10–12ft. in from either end. To be open grouted with a hand grouting plant.
 8.8.1945 Good.
23.3.1946 Good.
26.6.1949 Satisfactory.
26.3.1950 Satisfactory.
 4.5.1952 Satisfactory, slight repairs and pointing required to the arch and hounds (?) at each end.
 8.7.1953 Satisfactory, as 1952 but not urgent.

Reports on condition of Chipping Sodbury, 4444yds., 1932–1953. (Taken from official reports.)

27.11.1932 Good. A few straps on down pipes from garland gaiters require renewal – not urgent.
28.10.1934 Small patch of scaling near east end. A few of the straps to the down pipes from the garland gaiters require renewing and pipes and gutters should be tarred.
15.12.1935 Good.
22.11.1936 Good, a few additional hooks for the 1in. water pipes are required.
 5.12.1937 Good. Water coming through between 102 & 103 m.p.'s. Four additional down pipes will be fixed to lead water away.
13.11.1938 Brickwork good. Repairs required to 1½in. pipes, also garlands in 6 shafts should be tarred to preserve ironwork.

Repairs inside Chipping Sodbury tunnel, 23.5.1954 being carried out as a consequence of the 1952 inspection. This was one of the first times that mechanical aids had been available for re-pointing and it involved the use of a compressed air pump.

British Railways

31.3.1940 Good. Small repairs to down pipes and garlands, metal work must be tarred as soon as possible.
31.8.1941 Good.
8.8.1943 Good.
29.4.1945 Good. Down pipes at No. 4 shaft require attention.
31.3.1946 Good.

6.7.1947   Satisfactory.

26.6.1949   Satisfactory.

26.3.1950   Satisfactory. Slight development of movement in the arch at the Chipping Sodbury end noted. This is a circumferential fracture and a tendency for the portal to move out. No excessive water seepage. Leakage shown in No. 3 air shaft.

4.5.1952   Fairly satisfactory. Seepage of water into No. 3 air shaft which requires attention, also repairs required to garland and down pipes of No. 2 shaft. Slight movement in arch at Chipping Sodbury end. Pointing required over an area of 1,000sq.yds. between No. 3 shaft and Badminton end which will require single line working.

8.7.1953   Satisfactory. As 1952 but not urgent re No.3.. Garlands at air shafts and down pipes require attention.

The western entrance to Chipping Sodbury tunnel with a refuge provided in the side of the retaining wall. Similar refuges were located at regular intervals in both this and Alderton tunnel.

L.G.R.P.

APPENDIX G

Station reference numbers 1911.

(This was a system whereby each location (station, halt, depôt, yard, signalbox and receiving office or principle agency) on the GWR was identified by a number. It was intended to ensure accuracy of delivery of internal mail and correspondance.

1019 Wootton Bassett station.
1020 Wootton Bassett East 'box.
1021 Wootton Bassett West 'box.
1022 Brinkworth
1023 Little Somerford.
1024 Hullavington.
1025 Badminton.
1026 Chipping Sodbury.
1027 Westerleigh East Junction 'box.
1028 Westerleigh West Junction 'box.
1029 Coalpit Heath.
1030 Winterbourne.
1031 Stoke Gifford East 'box.
1032 Stoke Gifford West 'box.

Note: no reference number is shown as allocated to Westerleigh North S.B.